THE SPRING FEASTS

Activity Book

The Spring Feasts Activity Book

All rights reserved. By purchasing this Activity Book, the buyer is permitted to copy the activity sheets for personal and classroom use only, but not for commercial resale. With the exception of the above, this Activity Book may not be reproduced in whole or in part in any manner without written permission of the publisher.

Bible Pathway Adventures® is a trademark of BPA Publishing Ltd.

ISBN: 978-1-98-858592-5

Author: Pip Reid

Creative Director: Curtis Reid

For free Bible resources including coloring pages, worksheets, puzzles and more, visit our website at:

www.biblepathwayadventures.com

◆◇ INTRODUCTION ◇◆

Enjoy teaching your children the Biblical faith with our *Spring Feasts Activity Book*. This multi-level Activity Book contains a mix of worksheets, quizzes, creating writing activities, puzzles, and more! PLUS, scripture references for easy Bible verse look-up and an answer key for teachers. The perfect resource for Sabbath and Sunday School lessons, and homeschooling.

Bible Pathway Adventures helps educators around the world teach children the Biblical faith in a fun and creative way. We do this via our Activity Books, printable activities and Bible stories - available on our website www.biblepathwayadventures.com

Thanks for buying this Activity Book and supporting our ministry. Every book purchased helps us continue our work providing free Classroom Packs and discipleship resources to families and missions everywhere.

The search for Truth is more fun than Tradition!

★BONUS★
Our illustrated The Risen King storybook is available for download.
Type the link into your browser to get your FREE copy today!
https://BookHip.com/ZNJVLP

◇◆ TABLE OF CONTENTS ◆◇

Introduction 3
The Appointed Times 7

Passover & Feast of Unleavened Bread (Pesach and Chag HaMatzot)
Introduction: The Passover & Feast of Unleavened Bread 8
Bible quiz: The Ten Plagues 9
Map activity: Where is Egypt? 10
Worksheet: Ten Plagues of Egypt 11
Bible craft: Make a paper frog 12
Worksheet: I Spy! 13
Bible crossword: The Passover 14
Comprehension worksheet: The Passover meal 15
Bible word search: Unleavened Bread 16
Worksheet: What's the Word? 17
Coloring page: Preparing for the Passover 18
Worksheet: Learn to draw a sheep 19
Coloring page: The Passover 20
Worksheet: What do you eat for the Passover meal? 21
Worksheet: Unleavened Bread 22
Worksheet: The Exodus 23
Fact sheet: Unleavened Bread 24
Recipe: Let's Make Matzah! 25
Let's Learn Hebrew: Feast of Unleavened Bread 26
Complete the picture: Yeshua's last meal 28
Coloring page: The last meal 29
Worksheet: Pieces of Silver 30
Labyrinth: Before the Sanhedrin 31
Coloring worksheet: Yeshua before Pilate 32
Bible quiz: The Passover & Feast of Unleavened Bread 33
Worksheet: Garden of Gethsemane 34
Bible quiz: Death on the stake 35
Coloring worksheet: Crucifixion 36
Comprehension worksheet: The Temple 37

Worksheet: The Passover 38
Let's Write: The crucifixion 39
Bible verse copywork: The Passover lamb 40

Feast of First Fruits (Bikkurim)
Introduction: Feast of First Fruits 41
Worksheet: What's the Word? 42
Coloring page: Feast of First Fruits 43
Bible crossword: The cross and empty tomb 44
Coloring page: The temple 45
Coloring page: The High Priest 46
Worksheet: First Fruits offering 47
Let's Learn Hebrew: Bikkurim 48
Worksheet: First Fruits 50
Comprehension worksheet: Golgotha discovered? 51
Bible verse copywork: Feast of First Fruits 52
Bible quiz: The Resurrection 53
Bible word search: The Resurrection 54
Coloring worksheet: First Fruits 55
Finish the picture: He is Risen! 56
Crack the code: The resurrection 57
Worksheet: Disciple facts 58
Comprehension worksheet: The Romans 59
Question 'n color: The guard's report 60
Worksheet: What is a disciple? 61
Bible quiz: The twelve disciples 62
Worksheet: Yeshua has risen! 63
Worksheet: The Jerusalem News 64
Alphabet challenge 65
Comprehension worksheet: Who was Pontius Pilate? 66

Day of Pentecost (Shavu'ot)
Introduction: Shavu'ot 67
Coloring page: Ten Commandments 68
Bible quiz: The Ten Commandments 69
Bible activity: Dress like an Israelite 70
Question 'n color: Mount Sinai 71
Let's learn Hebrew: Shavu'ot 72

Comprehension worksheet: Mount Sinai 74
Coloring page: Twelve tribes of Israel 76
Bible quiz: Shavu'ot 77
Worksheet What's the Word? 78
Worksheet: Shavu'ot 79
Worksheet: The Israelites 80
Labyrinth: Pilgrimage to Jerusalem 81
Worksheet: My Travel Diary 82
Bible crossword: Shavu'ot 83
Coloring page: A mighty wind 84
Worksheet: The Holy Spirit 85
Worksheet: The Jerusalem News 86
Map activity: Twelve tribes of Israel 87
Coloring worksheet: Peter 88
Bible word search: Shavu'ot 89
Bible word scramble: How many people were baptized (mikvah'd)? 90

EXTRA ACTIVITIES
Bible verse copywork: The Ten Plagues 92

CRAFTS & PROJECTS
Bible craft: Make a paper plate lamb 103
Bible activity: Garden of Gethsemane 107
Worksheet: Who said it? 109
Bible activity: What goes inside the temple? 111
Bible craft: Make a paper plate tomb 117
Bible craft: Ten Commandments 121
Bible activity: Shavu'ot in Jerusalem 131
Worksheet: Let's learn about Shavu'ot 133
Bible craft: Appointed Time mobile 135

Answer Key 139
Discover more Activity Books! 143

THE APPOINTED TIMES

On His Biblical calendar, Yah has set aside special dates called Appointed Times. His Appointed Times (Mo'edim in Hebrew) all speak of the coming Messiah and the hope and plan of our Salvation. Many English language bibles use the word 'seasons' but the original Hebrew word is 'Mo'ed', which means 'appointed time'.

Some people believe these Appointed Times are Jewish Feasts. However, scripture tells us they are not Jewish or Hebrew Feasts; these are Yah's Appointed Times and are dress rehearsals for the whole House of Israel.

"These are the appointed feasts of Yah, the holy convocations, which you shall proclaim at the time appointed for them." (Leviticus 23:4)

The first set of Appointed Times were fulfilled with the first coming of Yeshua – the Feast of Unleavened Bread (including the Passover meal), Feast of First Fruits, and the Feast of Shavu'ot. The last set of Appointed Times will be fulfilled with the second coming of Yeshua – the Day of Trumpets, the Day of Atonement, the Feast of Tabernacles, and The Last Great Day.

THE PASSOVER & FEAST OF UNLEAVENED BREAD

When the Israelites left Egypt, they were in such a hurry that they did not have time to let their bread dough rise. So they carried the unbaked dough on their backs, and as they were walking, it cooked in the sun. Because the bread had no yeast, it became hard and flat, and was known as 'matzah'. Eating matzah every year during the Feast of Unleavened Bread reminds people of the Israelites' departure from Egypt and how Yah delivered them from bondage. Although the Israelites had been freed physically, they still worshipped the false gods of Egypt. They had to learn to leave Egypt spiritually.

The Hebrew name for the Feast of Unleavened Bread is Chag HaMatzot and literally means "Feast of the Unleavened Bread." It begins on the fifteenth day of Nissan (April) with the Passover meal, and lasts for seven days. Many people think this Feast is a Jewish celebration. But the Bible says that this Feast is one of Yah's 'Appointed Times'. The Passover points to Yeshua as our Passover lamb whose blood was shed for our sins. Yeshua was crucified on the day of preparation for the Passover at the same hour that the lambs were being slaughtered for the Passover meal that evening.

Color the Lamb!

"These are the feasts of Yah, holy convocations which you shall proclaim at their appointed times." (Leviticus 23:4)

THE TEN PLAGUES

Read Exodus 7:14-13:16.
Answer the questions below.

1. What was the first plague? ....

2. Egyptian magicians were able to copy which plagues? ....

3. What was the fourth plague? ....

4. Ashes were used in which plague? ....

5. What was the ninth plague? ....

6. What was the last plague? ....

7. How many plagues did Yah send on Egypt? ....

8. Who hardened Pharaoh's heart so he wouldn't free the Hebrews? ....

9. Whose bones did Moses take with him when he left Egypt? ....

10. The Hebrews left Egypt during which Appointed Time (Feast)? ....

WHERE IS EGYPT?

Follow the instructions below and mark the places on the map of Africa. You may need to use an atlas or the Internet to find the answers!

Color the king of Egypt

☐ Find and mark the land of Egypt

☐ Find and mark the Red Sea

☐ Draw the Nile River

Name four biblical characters who lived in Egypt:

.... , ... , ... , ...

TEN PLAGUES OF EGYPT

Read Exodus 7:14-11:10. Put the plagues in the correct order.
Write a number in the square for the order that it happened.

blood   livestock die   flies   lice

fiery hail   darkness   boils   frogs

locusts   death of firstborn

MAKE A PAPER FROG

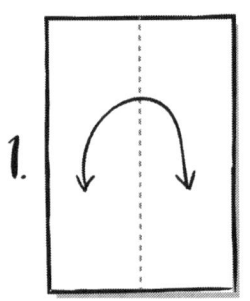 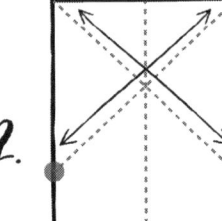 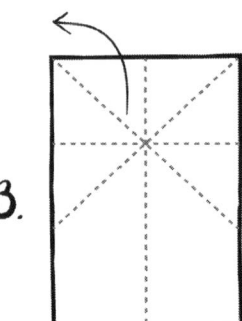 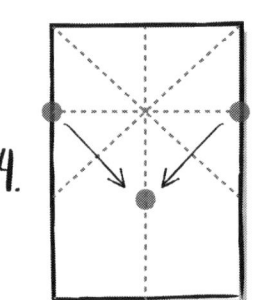 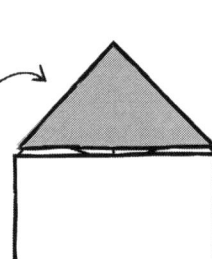

 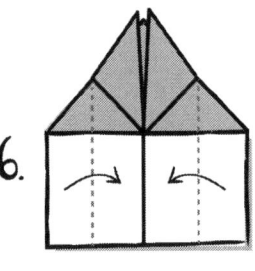 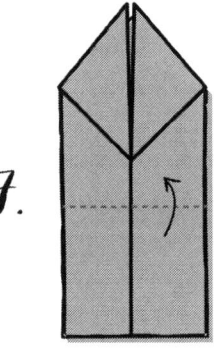 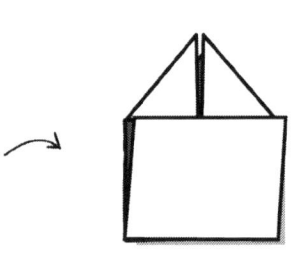

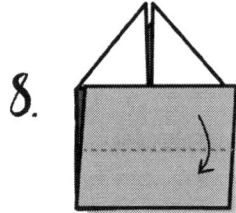 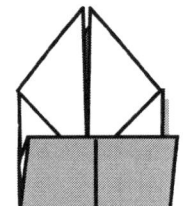 

1. Take a rectangle piece of paper, fold in half and open out again.
2. Fold both top corners to the opposite edge of the paper.
3. Where the diagonal creases meet in the middle, fold the paper backwards and open.
4. Hold the paper at the sides, then bring these points down to the center line and flatten.
5. Fold the uppermost triangles up to the top point.
6. Fold sides into the center crease.
7. Fold the bottom of the paper upwards so the end sits in the center of the top diamond.
8. Fold the same part downwards, in half.
9. Turn over. Ta-da! You have made a paper frog.

I SPY!

Yah sent ten plagues on the Egyptians. Can you name three of the plagues below?
Color the same plague a single color.
Then count each type of plague and write the number on the label.

THE PASSOVER

Read Exodus 12, Numbers 9, and John 19 (ESV).
Complete the crossword below.

ACROSS

2) A young sheep
4) Who led the Hebrews out of Egypt?
7) These things took place that the _____ might be fulfilled…" (John 19:36)
9) The Hebrews left Egypt during this Appointed Time. (Exodus 12:17)

DOWN

1) On the fourteenth day of the month at twilight is God's _____.
3) "They must not leave any lamb till morning or break any of its _____." (Numbers 9:12)
5) Jesus' Hebrew name
6) "…when I see the _____, I will pass over you…" (Exodus 12:13)
8) The king of Egypt
10) For seven days no _____ is to be found in your houses. (Exodus 12:19)

THE PASSOVER MEAL

According to the Bible, Moses followed Yah's instructions and asked Pharaoh to free the Hebrew slaves. When Pharaoh refused and ignored the nine plagues Yah had already sent, Yah decided to strike every firstborn in the land of Egypt. But first, He warned Moses that to protect their firstborn, the Hebrews should mark the two doorposts and lintel of their houses with lamb's blood. "When I see the blood, I will pass over you and no plague will befall you to destroy you, when I strike the land of Egypt." (Exodus 12:13)

After Yah led the Hebrews out of Egypt, He asked them to honor the Appointed Time of Unleavened Bread every year to remember how He protected them from His judgment on the Egyptians (Leviticus 23:4-8). Unleavened Bread starts on the fourteenth day of the Hebrew month of Nissan at sunset with a Passover meal. Today, believers of Yeshua honor the Passover meal by eating lamb and unleavened bread to remember the death of the Messiah.

Color the door

Why do you think Yah hardened Pharaoh's heart so he would not free the Hebrews?

....

Does your family eat the Passover meal every year? If so, what do you eat?

....

UNLEAVENED BREAD

Read Exodus 13 and Leviticus 23.
Find and circle each of the words from the list below.

```
B I T T E R H E R B S C Y C R T
R A Q Y H Y S S O P W A A O O M
U L W G A Q T A O I C I H N O X
P A S S O V E R J G K U W G B E
A P P O I N T E D T I M E R S G
S L X P V O Q H G P B A H E E Y
L E A V E N J Z O T W J N G V P
A U S M Y P I H P U E L D A E T
G E P B B B J F N L S I Y T N C
Y I W D T T L U V V Q E Y I D X
Q N S I Z M A O G E R U J O A Q
Q M A T Z A H X O U C H S N Y T
W P J V O W B M T D O P O G S V
U N L E A V E N E D B R E A D J
F F I Q C H Z H E B R E W S I S
G G E N E R A T I O N S I L B W
```

PASSOVER	LEAVEN	YAHWEH	BITTER HERBS
APPOINTED TIME	CONGREGATION	LAMB	GENERATIONS
BLOOD	MATZAH	HEBREWS	HYSSOP
EGYPT	HOUSE	UNLEAVENED BREAD	SEVEN DAYS

WHAT'S THE WORD?

Read Exodus 12:14-19. Fill in the blanks below.

"This day shall be a ……………… and you shall keep it as a feast to ………………: throughout your generations you shall keep it as feast ……………… .'"Seven days you shall eat ……………… bread; on the first day you shall put away ……………… out of your houses, for whoever eats leavened bread from the first day until the seventh day shall be cut off from ……………… . In the first day there shall be to you a holy ………………, and in the seventh day a holy convocation; no kind of ……………… shall be done except that which every man must eat that may only be done by you. You shall observe the ……………… ……………… of Unleavened Bread; for in this same day have I brought your armies out of the land of ………………: Therefore ……………… this day throughout your ……………… forever. In the first month, on the fourteenth day of the month at evening, you shall eat unleavened bread until the twenty first day of the month at evening."

MEMORIAL	YEAST	EGYPT
YAH	ISRAEL	GENERATIONS
FOREVER	CONVOCATION	WORK
UNLEAVENED	APPOINTED TIME	OBSERVE

"... take some **blood** and put it on the two doorposts and lintel of the **houses**..."

(Exodus 12:7)

LEARN TO DRAW SHEEP

During the first Passover meal in Egypt, the Hebrews ate lamb (a young sheep) and bitter herbs. Follow steps 1 – 6 and draw your own sheep!

1. 2. 3. 4. 5. 6. ta-da!

THE PASSOVER

The Israelites put blood on the two doorposts and lintel of their houses to protect them from the final plague. Read Exodus 12:1-30. Draw blood on the doorposts and lintel. Color the picture.

The Passover Meal

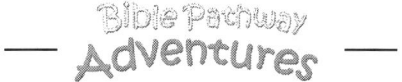

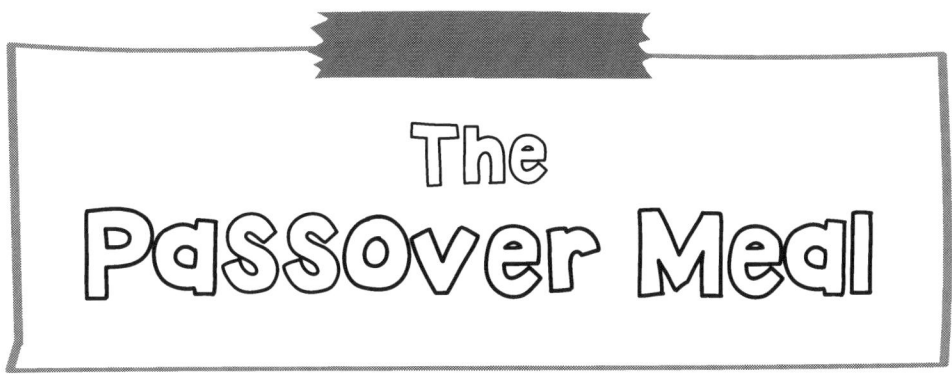

What do you eat for the Passover meal? Draw the food you eat on the plate below.

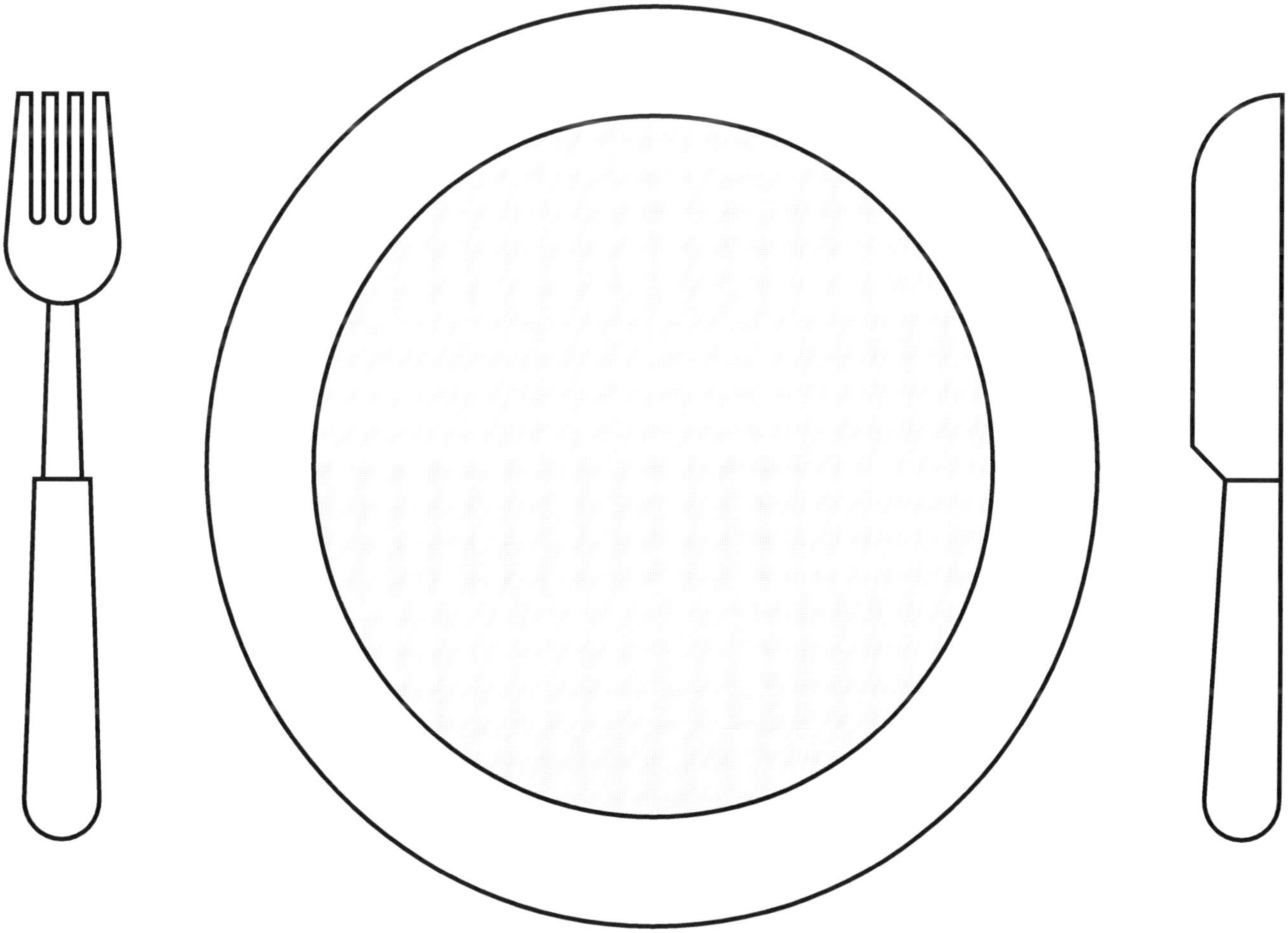

Unleavened Bread

Imagine you were in the crowd when Yeshua was crucified. What would you say to Him?

If the Ten Plagues of Egypt was a book, the cover would look like this...

Draw a picture of your family eating the Passover meal.

Where in the Bible can I find instructions to honor Unleavened Bread?

The EXODUS

The children of Israel left Egypt with their belongings. Think about life in ancient Egypt and make a list of items that may have been inside the Israelites' bags. Draw some of the items inside the bag.

1. ....
2. ....
3. ....
4. ....
5. ....
6. ....
7. ....
8. ....
9. ....
10. ....

UNLEAVENED BREAD

When the children of Israel left Egypt, they were in such a hurry that they did not have time to let their bread dough rise. So, they carried the unbaked dough on their backs. As they were walking, it cooked in the sun. Because the bread had no yeast, it became hard and flat, and was known as 'matzah'. Eating matzah every year during the Feast of Unleavened Bread reminds people of the Israelites' departure from Egypt and how God delivered them from bondage. Although the Israelites had been freed physically, they still worshipped the false gods of Egypt. They had to learn to leave Egypt spiritually. The Feast of Unleavened Bread begins on the fifteenth day of Nissan (March-April) and lasts for seven days. Many people think the Feast of Unleavened Bread is a Jewish celebration. But the Bible says that this Feast is one of God's 'Appointed Times.'

Color the matzah!

How do you and your family honor the Feast of Unleavened Bread?

In the Old Testament, how did Yah tell the Israelites to prepare their homes for this Feast? (Exodus 12:15-19)

LET'S MAKE MATZAH!

INGREDIENTS
1 cup all-purpose flour
1/3 cup vegetable oil
1/8 tsp salt
1/3 cup of water

METHOD
Line a baking sheet with parchment paper.
Mix flour, oil, and salt together in a bowl.
Add water and mix until dough is soft.
Using your hands, form dough into six balls and press into disks onto the prepared baking sheet.
Bake at 425°F (220°C) for 8-10 minutes or until bread is cooked.

✶ CHAG HAMATZOT ✶

The Hebrew words for Feast of Unleavened Bread are Chag HaMatzot. This Feast celebrates the journey of the children of Israel out of Egypt. Yah asks us to remember and honor this Appointed Time forever (Exodus 12:17).

Feast of Unleavened Bread

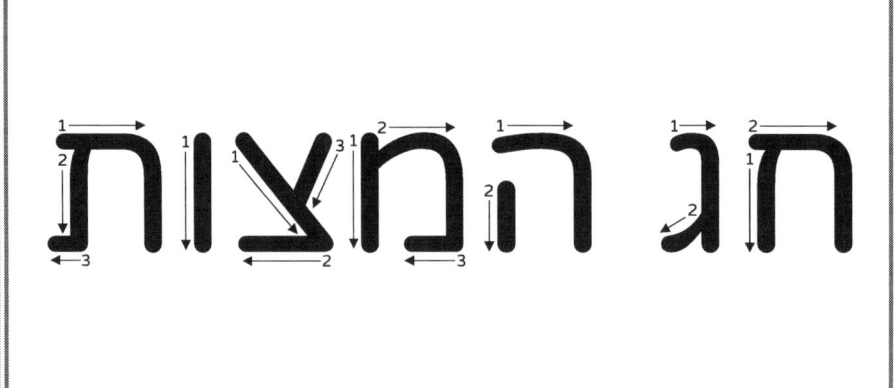

LET'S WRITE!

Practice writing 'Chag HaMatzot' on the lines below.

חג המצות

חג המצות

Try this on your own.
Remember that Hebrew is read from RIGHT to LEFT.

YESHUA'S LAST MEAL

Before Yeshua was crucified, He ate a meal with His disciples in an Upper Room in Jerusalem. Draw a scene from this story to complete the picture.

"This is my **body**, which is given for **you**. Do this in remembrance of **Me**."

(Luke 22:19)

PIECES OF SILVER

Count the number of silver coins in the bag to discover how much money Judas was given to betray Yeshua. Color the picture.

BEFORE THE SANHEDRIN

Before Yeshua was crucified, the Sanhedrin put him on trial.
The Sanhedrin had 71 members, including Caiaphas the high priest and other religious leaders.
Help the soldiers take Yeshua to the Sanhedrin.

YESHUA BEFORE PILATE

Open your Bibles and read Matthew 27.
Answer the questions. Color the picture.

1. How did Yeshua answer Pilate's questions? (verse 14)

....
....
....
....

2. Who sent Pilate a message? (verse 19)

....
....
....
....

3. Who did Pilate hand over to be crucified? (verse 26)

....
....
....
....

www.biblepathwayadventures.com
The Spring Feasts Activity Book

THE PASSOVER & FEAST OF UNLEAVENED BREAD

Read Exodus 13, 2 Chronicles 30 & 35, John 6, Acts 20, and 1 Corinthians 5 & 15.
Answer the questions below.

1. Which Feast did Paul encourage people to keep in 1 Cor 5? ....

2. What type of bread did the Hebrews take when they left Egypt? ....

3. How long is the Feast of Unleavened Bread? ....

4. The Passover meal takes place at the start of which Feast? ....

5. How long were the Israelites told to observe the Passover meal? ....

6. Which Israelite king honored this Feast in 2 Chronicles 30? ....

7. In which city did Josiah honor this Feast? ....

8. After the Feast of Unleavened Bread, where did Paul sail in Acts 20:6? ....

9. How many people did Yeshua feed before this Feast in John 6? ....

10. Yeshua rose from the grave on which Appointed Time during the Feast of Unleavened Bread? ....

THE OLIVE TREE

Yeshua spent time with His disciples in the Garden of Gethsemane. The name Gethsemane means 'oil press'. Today, olive presses can still be found throughout the land of Israel. The Hebrews made olive oil by placing olives in sacks and stacking them on top of one another. A beam was lowered onto the stack and weight added to the end of the beam to press oil from the olives. Label the olive tree from the words below. Color the tree.

- Roots
- Branches
- Olives
- Leaves
- Trunk

DEATH ON THE STAKE

Read Matthew 27:32-56.
Answer the questions below.

1. Who sentenced Yeshua to die?

2. Who was forced to carry Yeshua's crossbeam through the streets of Jerusalem?

3. At what place was Yeshua nailed to the stake?

4. What was written on the sign above Yeshua's head?

5. What did Yeshua cry out while he was nailed to the stake?

6. Who was crucified next to Yeshua?

7. After Yeshua died, how long did darkness cover the land?

8. Who asked Pilate for Yeshua's body?

9. What did the Roman soldier use to pierce Yeshua's side?

10. What was Yeshua wrapped in before he was buried?

Crucifixion

Read Matthew 27:50-52 and write the Bible verse below.

....

....

....

1. What tore into two pieces when Yeshua gave up His spirit?

....

....

2. What shook the city after Yeshua died?

....

....

3. Who said, "Surely He was the Son of God!"?

....

....

Draw your favorite scene from this story.

What could the life of Yeshua teach me?	God used Yeshua to...

THE TEMPLE

The Temple in Jerusalem was the center of Hebrew life during biblical times. It began with the construction of the first temple by King Solomon, and ended with its destruction by the Romans in 70 AD. To house the Ark of the Covenant, King Solomon built the first temple in the tenth century, which was later destroyed by the Babylonians. A second temple was built during the time of Nehemiah and underwent major renovation during the reign of King Herod.

Every year during the Passover sacrifice at the Temple, those who wanted to sacrifice a lamb formed groups. Each group slaughtered one Passover lamb for that group of people. The priests allowed the Court of the Israelites to be filled three times to do this. The Passover lamb, unlike the usual animal offerings, was sacrificed by the Israelites themselves. The lambs were roasted and eaten that night.

Color the temple!

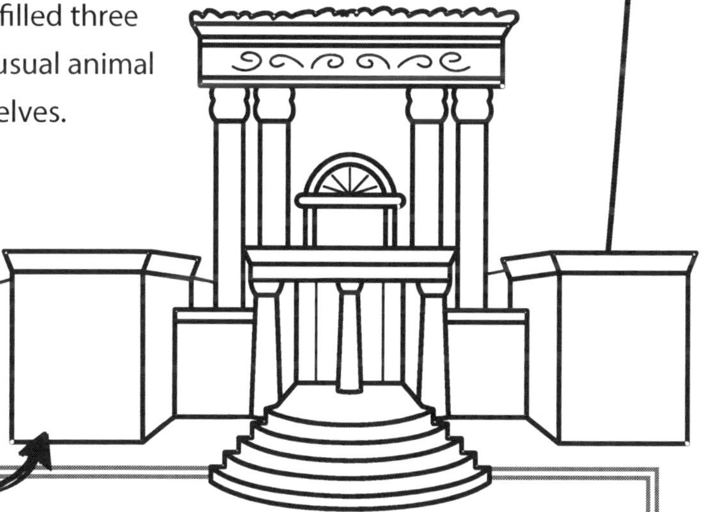

Who built the first temple in Jerusalem?

....

In biblical times, how did the Israelites slaughter a lamb for the Passover meal?

....

THE PASSOVER

Read Exodus 12, Matthew 26, and John 18.
Discuss how the pictures below relate to the Passover and the story of the crucifixion.
Match each word with the correct picture.

Bread **Lamb** **Olive tree**

Passover **High Priest**

Let's Write

Read the story of the crucifixion (Matthew 27:27-44, Mark 15:16-32, Luke 23:26-43, and John 19:16-27). Write the story in your own words on the lines below.

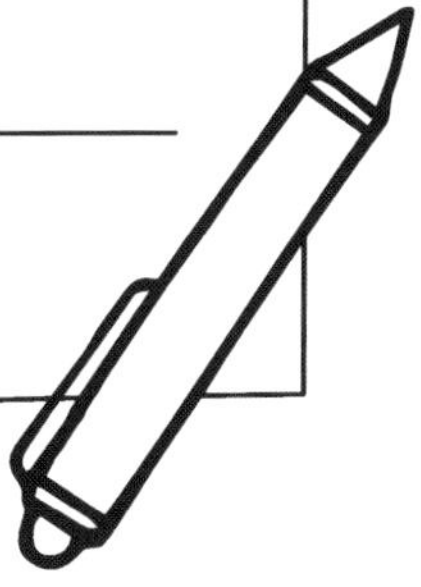

THE PASSOVER LAMB

Open your Bible to 1 Corinthians 5:7. Copy the scripture on the lines provided. Use your imagination to color the illustration at the bottom of the page.

FEAST OF FIRST FRUITS

The Appointed Time of Unleavened Bread was a busy time in Jerusalem. Between 250,000 to 500,000 pilgrims came to keep the Feast. Some slept in Jerusalem, while others stayed in nearby villages or in tents around the city. Pilgrims visited the Temple, listened to teachers, and bought gifts to take home. There was a great deal of activity, festivity, and many opportunities to make new friends and renew old friendships.

During this time, the Feast of First Fruits offering took place. It fell on the day after the Sabbath during Unleavened Bread. First Fruits is one of Yah's Appointed Times, and in Yeshua's day it was the first harvest of the spring. It was the job of the High Priest to wave the first sheaf (usually a barley cluster known as the first of the first fruits) before Yah at the Temple, with accompanying sacrifices. Only after this ceremony could Israelites harvest the fruit and grain they had grown.

First Fruits points to Yeshua's resurrection as the first fruits of the righteous. He was resurrected on this very day, which is a reason that Paul the Apostle refers to Him as the 'first fruits from the dead.'

Color the barley!

"But in fact Yeshua has been raised from the dead, the firstfruits of those who have fallen asleep." (1 Corinthians 15:20)

WHAT'S THE WORD?

Read Leviticus 23:9-12. Fill in the blanks below.

" ………………… spoke to ……………………, saying, "Speak to the children of ……………………… and tell them, 'When you have come into the land which I give to you and reap its ……………………, then you shall bring the sheaf of the …………………… …………………… of your harvest to the …………………… and he shall wave the sheaf before Yah, to be accepted for you. On the next day after the …………………… the priest shall wave it. On the day when you wave the ……………………, you shall offer a male …………………… without defect a year old for a burnt …………………… to Yah. "

YAHWEH SHEAF
ISRAEL LAMB
HARVEST MOSES
OFFERING FIRST FRUITS
SABBATH PRIEST

Feast of First Fruits

THE CROSS AND EMPTY TOMB

Read Matthew 28, Mark 16, Luke 24, John 20, and Acts 1 (ESV).
Complete the crossword below.

ACROSS

4) Name of the place where Yeshua was crucified.
7) The Roman governor who sentenced Yeshua to die.
8) This type of spiritual being opened the tomb.
9) Yeshua rose from the grave on which Appointed Time?

DOWN

1) After Yeshua died, this shook the city.
2) Yeshua was crucified on this Roman device.
3) Beside which sea did Yeshua meet His disciples after He rose from the grave?
5) The disciple who betrayed Yeshua.
6) What was torn from top to bottom inside the temple?
7) This disciple jumped out of the boat and swam toward Yeshua.

THE TEMPLE

During the Feast of First Fruits, the High Priest waved a sheaf of barley before Yah at the temple. Color the temple.

The High Priest

These are the garments they are to make: a breastpiece, an ephod, a robe, a woven tunic, a turban and a sash. They are to make these sacred garments for your brother Aaron and his sons, so they may serve me as priests.

(Exodus 28:4)

FIRST FRUIT OFFERING

During the Feast of First Fruits, the ancient Israelites took the first fruit of their Spring harvest and offered it to Yah. This way, they sanctified their whole harvest (Leviticus 23:9-14). What do you give Yah on the Feast of First Fruits?
Draw a picture of your gift in the space below.

✡ BIKKURIM ✡

The Hebrew word for Feast of First Fruits is Bikkurim. During the Feast of First Fruits in ancient Israel, the Israelites took the first fruit of their Spring harvest and offered it to Yah. Yah asked us to remember and honor this Appointed Time forever.

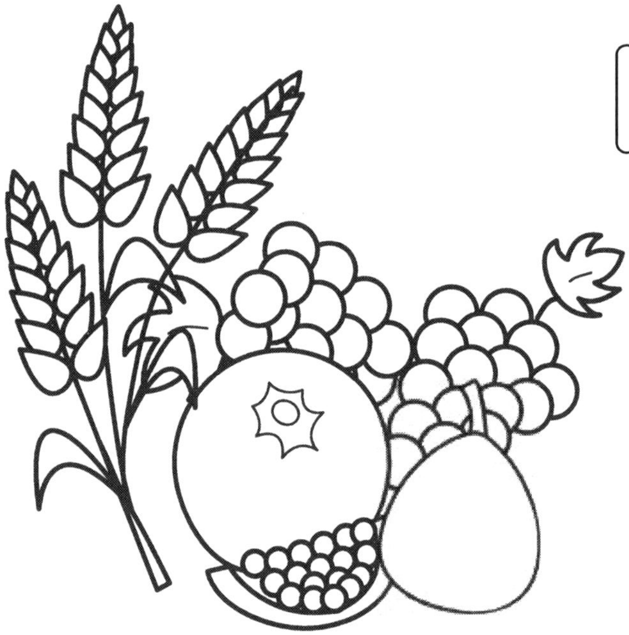

Bikkurim

בִּכּוּרִים

Feast of First Fruits

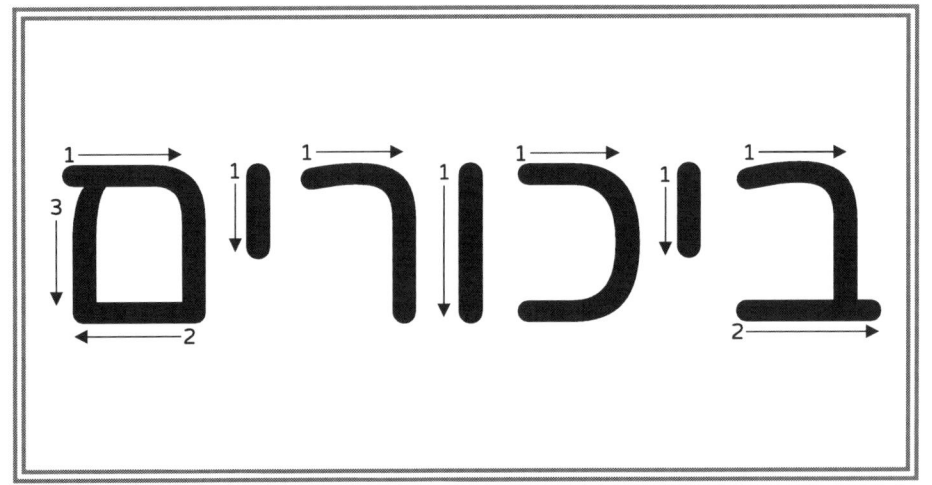

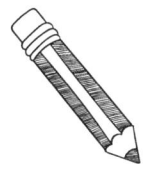 # LET'S WRITE!

Practice writing the word 'Bikkurim' on the lines below.

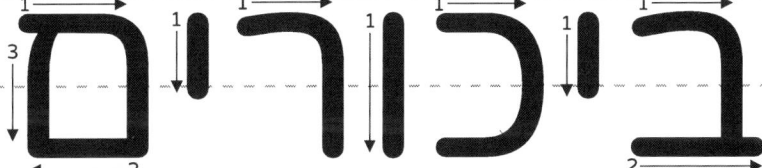

ביכורים

Try this on your own.
Remember that Hebrew is read from RIGHT to LEFT.

First Fruits

Imagine you are Mary. What would you say to the disciples when you returned from the empty tomb?

Where in the Bible can I find instructions to honor First Fruits?

Draw a picture of the angel opening the tomb.

If the resurrection was a movie, the movie poster would look like this...

GOLGOTHA DISCOVERED?

According to the Bible, Yeshua was crucified outside the walls of Jerusalem near a place called "Golgotha" or the "Place of the Skull" (Mark 15:22). Jewish law did not permit crucifixions and burials inside the city. Because dead bodies were considered unclean, Hebrew burial plots and cemeteries were always outside the city walls.

Some archaeologists believe they have found Yeshua's crucifixion site just outside the old walls of Jerusalem at Golgotha. It is located next to a bus stop near the tomb where Yeshua was laid. The actual crucifixion site was under many feet of soil, with holes in the rock where crosses were erected, and niches in the rock wall behind where signs were placed. The central cross-hole had an earthquake crack beside it. The Bible mentions that an earthquake occurred during the crucifixion, causing rocks to split. "And behold, the curtain of the temple was torn in two, from top to bottom. And the earth shook and the rocks were split." (Matthew 27:51) What do you think? Have archaeologists found the site of Yeshua's crucifixion?

Color the Hebrew!

What is another name for Golgotha?

....

What have archaeologists discovered near the walls of Jerusalem?

....

FEAST OF FIRST FRUITS

Open your Bible to Matthew 28:5-6. Copy the scriptures on the lines provided. Use your imagination to color the illustration at the bottom of the page.

THE RESURRECTION

Read Matthew 28, Mark 16, Luke 24, John 20, and Acts 1.
Answer the questions below.

1. Who rolled away Yeshua's tomb stone? ....

2. During which Appointed Time was Yeshua raised from the grave? ....

3. What did the priests give the Roman guards to keep quiet? ....

4. Which woman met Yeshua outside the tomb? ....

5. When Mary Magdalene, Mary mother of James, and Salome went to the tomb with their spices, what did they find? ....

6. What did the two strangers say to the women outside the tomb? ....

7. Which disciple doubted Yeshua was alive? ....

8. While they waited for Yeshua, His disciples went fishing on which Sea? ....

9. How long did Yeshua stay on earth after His resurrection before He rose to Heaven? ....

10. What were Yeshua's final instructions to His disciples? ....

THE RESURRECTION

Read Matthew 28, Mark 16, Luke 24, John 20, and Acts 1.
Find and circle each of the words from the list below.

ANGEL	GUARDS	TOMB	UNLEAVENED BREAD
APPOINTED TIME	MESSIAH	GARDEN	DISCIPLES
PETER	FIRST FRUITS	GALILEE	YESHUA
RISEN	STONE	MARY	JERUSALEM

First Fruits

Read Matthew 28:7 and write the Bible verse below.

....

....

....

1. Who rolled away the stone? (Matthew 28:2)

....

....

2. Yeshua first appeared to whom outside His tomb? (John 20:16)

....

....

3. Who did Mary tell that Yeshua had risen? (John 20:18)

....

....

Draw your favorite scene from this story.

What could Yeshua's resurrection teach me?	I honor First Fruits by…

HE IS RISEN!

Yeshua rose from the grave on the Feast of First Fruits. Beside the tomb, draw the angel and two Roman soldiers. Color the picture.

THE RESURRECTION!

Did Yeshua tell the disciples that He would be raised from the grave? Let's find out! The Bible verse below is written in code. Use the chart at the bottom of the page to fill in the missing letters and crack the code! *Hint: Read Luke 24:6 (ESV)*

"He is not here, but has risen. Remember how he told you, while he was still in Galilee,"

DISCIPLE FACTS

Yeshua taught His disciples how to disciple others. Who were Yeshua's disciples? Read the facts below and match them with the correct disciple.

1. .... A Judean, betrayed Yeshua for 30 pieces of silver, hung himself.

2. .... Greek name was Didymus, doubted the resurrection of Yeshua.

3. .... Brother of James, second name was Boanerges, which means son of Thunder, wrote the Gospel of John & the book of Revelation.

4. .... Came from Bethsaida, one of the first disciples.

5. .... Son of Zebedee, preached in Jerusalem & Judea, was beheaded by Herod in AD 44.

6. .... Brother of Peter, fisherman, originally a disciple of John the Baptist.

7. .... Tax-collector, also called Levi.

8. .... Brother of James the Younger, he asked Yeshua at the Last Supper, "Why do you intend to show yourself to us and not to the world?" (John 14:22)

9. .... His name means Son of Tolmai, lived in Cana.

10. .... Fisherman, married, denied knowing Yeshua three times.

ANDREW JUDAS
BARTHOLOMEW JUDE (OR THADDEUS)
JAMES, SON OF ZEBEDEE MATTHEW
THOMAS PETER
JOHN PHILIP

THE ROMANS

The Romans conquered Jerusalem in 63 BC and ruled Judea for many years. They used local leaders like Herod the Great to control the people. Roman brutality was a part of life. For example, a Roman soldier could force a person to carry whatever needed moving for one mile. The Romans also used crucifixion as a way to control everyone. Often you would see roads lined with people crucified on crosses because they had opposed Caesar, the Roman emperor.

The Romans charged the Hebrews all types of taxes, including food, road, and poll taxes. They also faced religious taxes and other taxes imposed by Herod. There were water, house, and sales taxes, and extra taxes on items such as meat and salt. There was also a temple tax to pay for the maintenance of the temple in Jerusalem. Because of these taxes, many Hebrew families were very poor. In 66 AD, the people finally had enough of the Romans. They fought the Romans until the Romans captured Jerusalem and destroyed the Temple in 70 AD.

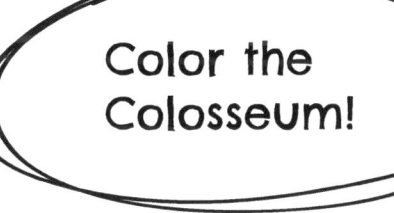

How did the Romans control the people of Judea?

....

What type of taxes did the Hebrews have to pay?

....

www.biblepathwayadventures.com
The Spring Feasts Activity Book

THE GUARD'S REPORT

Open your Bibles and read Matthew 28.
Answer the questions. Color the picture.

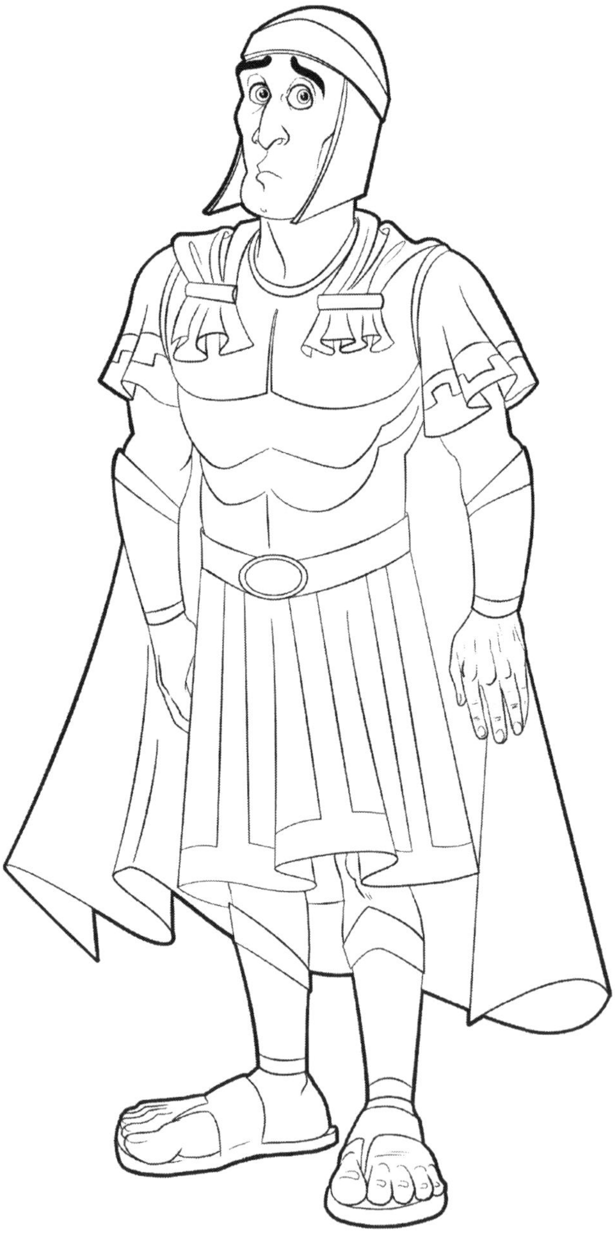

1. Who told the religious leaders that Yeshua was gone? (verse 11)

....
....
....
....

2. What did the religious leaders give the soldiers to keep quiet? (verse 12)

....
....
....
....

3. What did the religious leaders tell the soldiers to say about Yeshua's disappearance? (verse 13)

....
....
....
....

What is a disciple?

Yeshua had twelve disciples. Their names were Simon Peter, Andrew, James (son of Zebedee), John, Philip, Bartholomew, Thomas, Matthew, James (son of Alphaeus), Thaddaeus, Simon the Zealot and Judas Iscariot. (Matthew 10:1-4 and Luke 6:12-16.)
Let's learn what it means to be a disciple.

Before the time of Yeshua, discipleship was already a well-established process within Hebrew culture. To become a disciple, you first had to finish Bet Midrash. This was where boys aged 13-15 studied the entire Tanakh (Old Testament) while learning the family trade. Boys who finished Bet Midrash were then invited by a teacher to become his disciple. These disciples were known as talmidim and they learned everything from their teacher. They ate the same food as their teacher ate, they learned to keep the Sabbath the way their teacher kept the Sabbath, and they studied the Torah exactly the same way as their teacher. A disciple had four jobs; to memorize his teacher's words, to learn his teacher's traditions and interpretations, to imitate his teacher, and after he was fully trained, he would become a teacher and teach disciples of his own.

"Every disciple fully trained will be like his teacher." (Luke 6:40)

I imitate Yeshua everyday by...

....

....

....

....

Color the disciple! ➡

www.biblepathwayadventures.com
The Spring Feasts Activity Book

© BPA Publishing Ltd 2020

THE TWELVE DISCIPLES

Read Matthew 4, 10, 14, 21, 28, Luke 9, 22, and John 13, 19.
Answer the questions below.

1. Which disciple was a tax collector? ....

2. Who were the first two disciples to be called? ....

3. Which disciple tried to walk on water, like Yeshua? ....

4. After which meal did the disciples sing a psalm? ....

5. Which disciple betrayed Yeshua? ....

6. What event did Peter, James and John witness on a mountain with Yeshua? ....

7. What did Yeshua do to each disciple during the Last Supper? ....

8. Which disciple looked after Mary after Yeshua's death? ....

9. What was Yeshua's final commission to His disciples? ....

10. What did Yeshua send two disciples to fetch on His triumphal entry into Jerusalem? ....

YESHUA HAS RISEN!

Based on 1 Corinthians 15:20.
Read the Bible verse, then trace and write the bible verse on the lines below.

Yeshua has risen from the dead, the first fruits of those who are sleeping.

Try writing this sentence on your own.

City of Jerusalem

The Jerusalem News

FEAST OF FIRST FRUITS   A BIBLE HISTORY PUBLICATION

Mary's story!

....

....

....

....

....

....

Tomb found empty!

....

....

....

....

Barley harvest starts

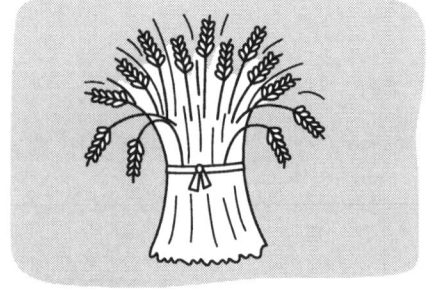

Alphabet challenge

Can you find a word in the Bible for each letter of the alphabet?

A.. N..
B.. O..
C.. P..
D.. Q..
E.. R..
F.. S.. 
G.. T..
H.. U..
I.. V..
J.. W..
K.. X..
L.. Y..
M.. Z..

WHO WAS PONTIUS PILATE?

This article introduces Pontius Pilate. As you read it, think about the type of man who sentenced Yeshua to die. Answer the questions below.

Pontius Pilate

At the time of Yeshua's death, Pontius Pilate was the Roman governor of Judea and Samaria. His job was to collect taxes, build roads, and govern this region of the Roman Empire. Pilate was not a popular governor. In a letter from Agrippa I, Pilate was accused of harsh behavior, pride, violence, greed, holding executions without trial, and horrible cruelty. In 36 AD, three years after he sentenced Yeshua to death, Pilate was called back to Rome for questioning about harsh management of an incident involving the Jewish people. Some historians claim that Pilate later committed suicide. Others say Emperor Nero executed him. Another tradition says that He finally accepted Yeshua and was executed by Emperor Tiberius.

In 1961, archaeologists found a limestone block in an ancient Roman amphitheater near Caesarea-on-the-Sea (Maritima). On its face is an inscription, part of a larger dedication to Tiberius Caesar, which says that it was from "Pontius Pilate, Prefect of Judea." Visitors to Caesarea today see a replica limestone block since the original is in the Israel Museum in Jerusalem.

Questions:

Why was Pilate an unpopular governor?

....

What did archaeologists find that proves Pilate once governed Judea?

....

SHAVU'OT

Fifty days from the day the first fruits of the barley harvest were waved before Yah, is Shavu'ot or the Day of Pentecost. Shavu'ot is one of Yah's Appointed Times and is also known as the Feast of Weeks. During the time of Yeshua, it was one of three Appointed Times that Israelite men were expected to travel to Jerusalem to honor.

This time of year marks the start of the wheat harvest and the end of the barley harvest. Shavu'ot also marks the time the Twelve Tribes of Israel were given the Ten Commandments on Mount Sinai. And so the nation of Israel was established. Peter and the disciples were in Jerusalem to keep the Feast of Shavu'ot when tongues like fire descended, and many pilgrims understood what the disciples were saying in their own language. Some Bible scholars believe these pilgrims were descendants of the ten tribes of Israel scattered abroad.

Color the Israelite!

"You shall count seven full weeks from the day after the Sabbath, from the day that you brought the sheaf of the wave offering. You shall count fifty days to the day after the seventh Sabbath. Then you shall present a grain offering of new grain to Yahweh." (Leviticus 23:15-16)

The Ten Commandments

THE TEN COMMANDMENTS

Read Exodus 20.
Answer the questions below.

1. To whom did Yah give the Ten commandments? ....

2. What is the 5th commandment? ....

3. 'Thou shalt not kill' is which commandment? ....

4. What were the Ten Commandments written on? ....

5. What is the 4th commandment? ....

6. Which commandment instructs us not to lie? ....

7. Which commandment forbids stealing? ....

8. Which commandment forbids making idols to worship Yah? ....

9. Where did Moses receive the commandments from Yah? ....

10. What is the 10th commandment? ....

DRESS LIKE AN ISRAELITE

The ancient Israelites wore clothing like tunics and robes.
Let's make a tunic! Ask your parents to help you do this.

Instructions:

1. Parents - measure your child's body from elbow to elbow and knee to shoulder.
2. Find an old blanket or sheet as big as your child and fold it in half.
3. Cut a slit in the middle of the fold wide enough to fit their head.
4. Place the 'tunic' over their head. Tie a belt made from rope, ribbon, leather, or cloth around their waist.

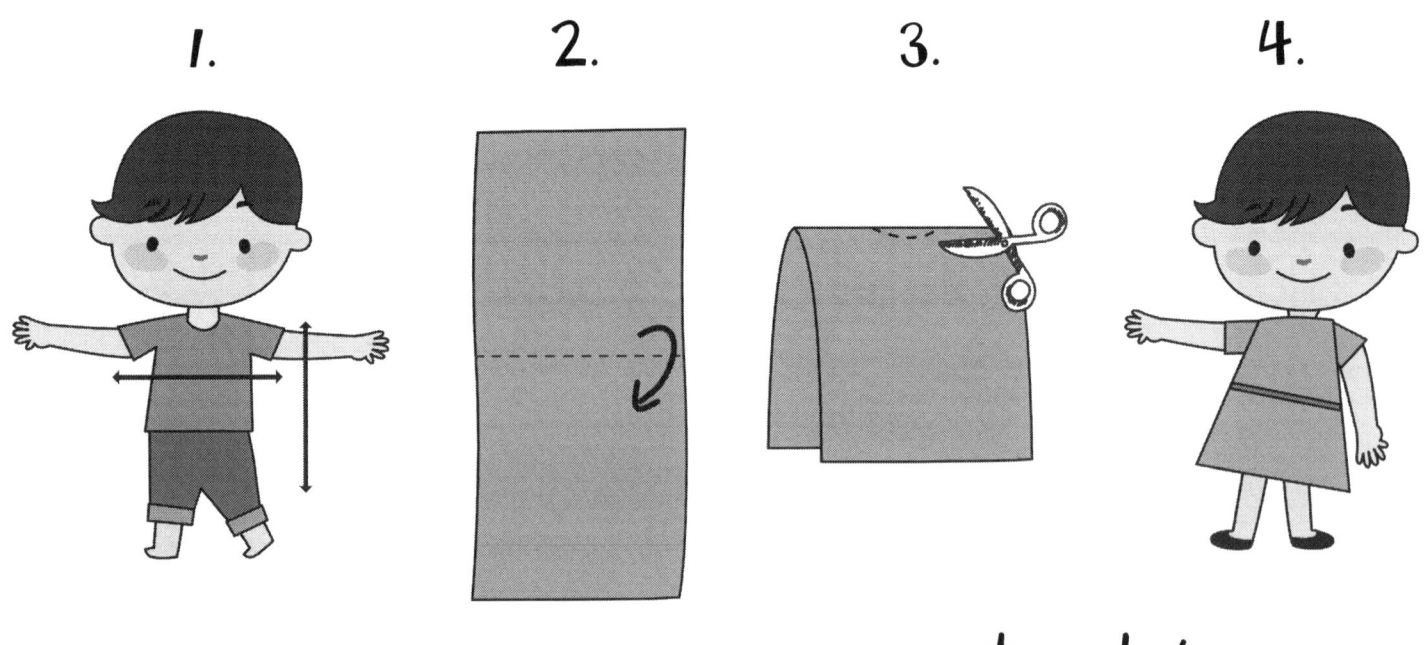

MOUNT SINAI

Open your Bibles and read Exodus 20:1-21.
Answer the questions. Color the picture.

1. What day should we keep holy (set-apart)? (verse 8)

....
....
....
....

2. Who should we honor? (verse 12)

....
....
....
....

3. Why did the Israelites want Moses to speak to them? (verse 19)

....
....
....
....

www.biblepathwayadventures.com
The Spring Feasts Activity Book

© BPA Publishing Ltd 2020

71

SHAVU'OT

The Hebrew word for Day of Pentecost is Shavu'ot. At the time of Yeshua, Israelites from different countries came to Jerusalem to honor this Feast. Some people believe these Israelites were of the ten 'lost' tribes of Israel that Yah had scattered all over the earth many years ago.

Shavu'ot

שָׁבוּעוֹת

Day of Pentecost

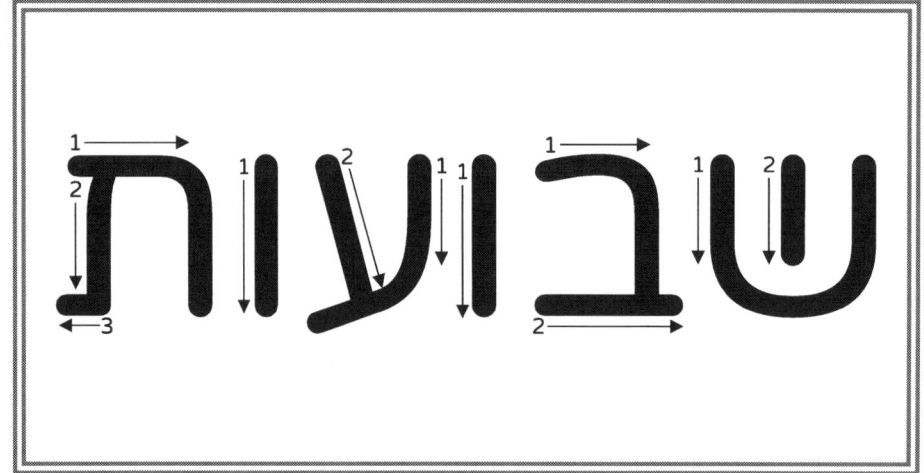

Practice writing 'Shavu'ot' on the lines below.

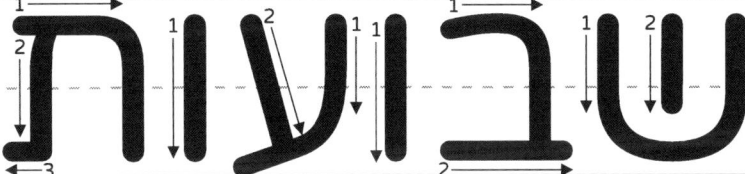

שבועות

Try this on your own.
Remember that Hebrew is read from RIGHT to LEFT.

MOUNT SINAI

Many people believe Mount Sinai is located on the Sinai Peninsula in Egypt. But there is no scriptural or archaeological evidence that supports this place as the biblical Mount Sinai. Let's take a closer look and see if you agree. Read the article and answer the questions on the next page.

Mount Sinai

Did you know that the Bible says that Mount Sinai is located in Arabia, not the land of Egypt (Galatians 4:25)? Recently, archaeologists discovered a place that points to Jebel el Lawz in Saudi Arabia as the location of the biblical Mount Sinai. This mountain is located in northwest Saudi Arabia near the coast of the Gulf of Aqaba. An aerial map shows the mountain to be an almost semi-circular shape, enclosing an area of 5,000 acres. Unlike other mountains nearby, the entire top of Jebel el Lawz is blackened (Ex 19:18). On the face of Jebel el Lawz is evidence of an ancient stream. The Bible says that when Moses destroyed the golden calf, he "cast the dust into the brook that descended out of the mount…" (Deut 9:21). In 1985, archaeologists found many large stone columns (or wells) nearby that formed a line along an ancient "lake" area bordering the holy precinct. Were these wells and lake part of a water supply system created to provide the Israelites with fresh water?

The Bible says, "Moses…built an altar under the hill, and twelve pillars according to the twelve tribes of Israel" (Ex 24:4). At the base of Jebel el Lawz, archaeologists found an altar similar to the altar of "uncut" stone mentioned in the book of Exodus (Ex 20:25; 24:4). Beside the altar was an 'L' shaped structure with walls about three feet thick. Was this the area where animals were killed before being sacrificed as a burnt offering? Nearby, archaeologists found twelve large granite boulders about six feet wide and nine feet tall. Approximately 2km away from the holy precinct archaeologists discovered a large stone altar with inscriptions of Egyptian animal fertility gods. If the Israelites created these inscriptions, then it makes sense they depicted Egyptian gods since they used to live in Egypt.

Homework

Mission objective: To understand the location of the biblical Mount Sinai. Read each question and write your answer on the lines below.

Look at an atlas. Where is Saudi Arabia?

....

....

Read the passage on the previous page, and also do your own research. What evidence have archaeologists found that points to Jebel el Lawz as the biblical Mount Sinai?

....

....

What do you think? Is Jebel el Lawz the biblical Mount Sinai?

....

....

TWELVE TRIBES OF ISRAEL

Read Leviticus 23:15-22. Yah asked the House of Israel to honor Shavu'ot forever. In the House of Israel there are twelve tribes. The High Priest wears a breastplate with twelve gemstones, each stone representing one of the tribes of Israel. Color the picture.

SHAVU'OT

Read Exodus 19-20, Leviticus 23, Deuteronomy 16, and Acts 2-3. Answer the questions below.

1. From which mountain did Yah give His commandments? ....

2. How long did Moses stay on the mountain to receive the commandments? ....

3. How many tribes camped at the foot of the mountain? ....

4. What is the fourth commandment? ....

5. What is the fifth commandment? ....

6. In Acts 2, what sound did the disciples hear when they arrived at the temple? ....

7. What did the people hear when the disciples began speaking to them? ....

8. Which disciple spoke to the people about Yeshua? ....

9. In Acts 2:41, how many people repented and were baptized that day? ....

10. How many days after Yeshua rose into Heaven did the disciples celebrate Shavu'ot? ....

WHAT'S THE WORD?

Read Acts 2:1-11. Fill in the blanks below.

"Now when the day of .... had come, they were all in one place. Suddenly there came from the sky a sound like a rushing mighty ...., and it filled the entire house where they were sitting. Tongues like .... appeared and were distributed to them, and one sat on each of them. They were all filled with the .... and began to speak in other ...., as the Spirit gave them the ability to speak. Now there were staying in Jerusalem Israelites, devout men, from every .... under the sky. When this sound was heard, the crowd came together and were surprised, because everyone .... the apostles speaking in his own language. They were all amazed, saying to one another, "Aren't these men who speak from the ....? How do we hear everyone in our own native language? ...., Medes, Elamites, and people from ...., Judea, Cappadocia, Pontus, Asia, Phrygia, Pamphylia, ..., the parts of Libya around Cyrene, visitors from Rome, both Jews and proselytes, Cretans and ....: we hear them speaking in our languages the mighty works of Yah!"

PENTECOST	LANGUAGES	PARTHIANS
WIND	NATION	MESOPOTAMIA
FIRE	HEARD	EGYPT
HOLY SPIRIT	GALILEE	ARABIANS

Shavu'ot

If the Day of Pentecost was a book, the cover would look like this...

Imagine you are a Parthian visiting Jerusalem. What would you think when you heard the apostles speak in your own language?

Draw a picture of Moses receiving the Ten Commandments.

If you were suddenly able to understand every language, how would your life change?

THE ISRAELITES

On the day of Pentecost, men from many nations were in Jerusalem. The city streets were crowded with pilgrims. Some Bible scholars believe these pilgrims were of the ten tribes of Israel that Yah had scattered among the nations. Read Acts 2:1-3. Write ten nationalities in the boxes below. Color the pilgrim.

PILGRIMAGE TO JERUSALEM

The Day of Pentecost was a great harvest celebration.
Help the pilgrims get to Jerusalem to celebrate Shavu'ot at the temple.

MY TRAVEL DIARY

Imagine you are a Parthian visiting Jerusalem to celebrate the Day of Pentecost. What did you see? Keep a record of your visit.

I learned...

I Heard...

Best thing I ate...

I found...

The strangest thing I saw was...

SHAVU'OT

Read Acts 2:1-38 (ESV). Complete the crossword below.

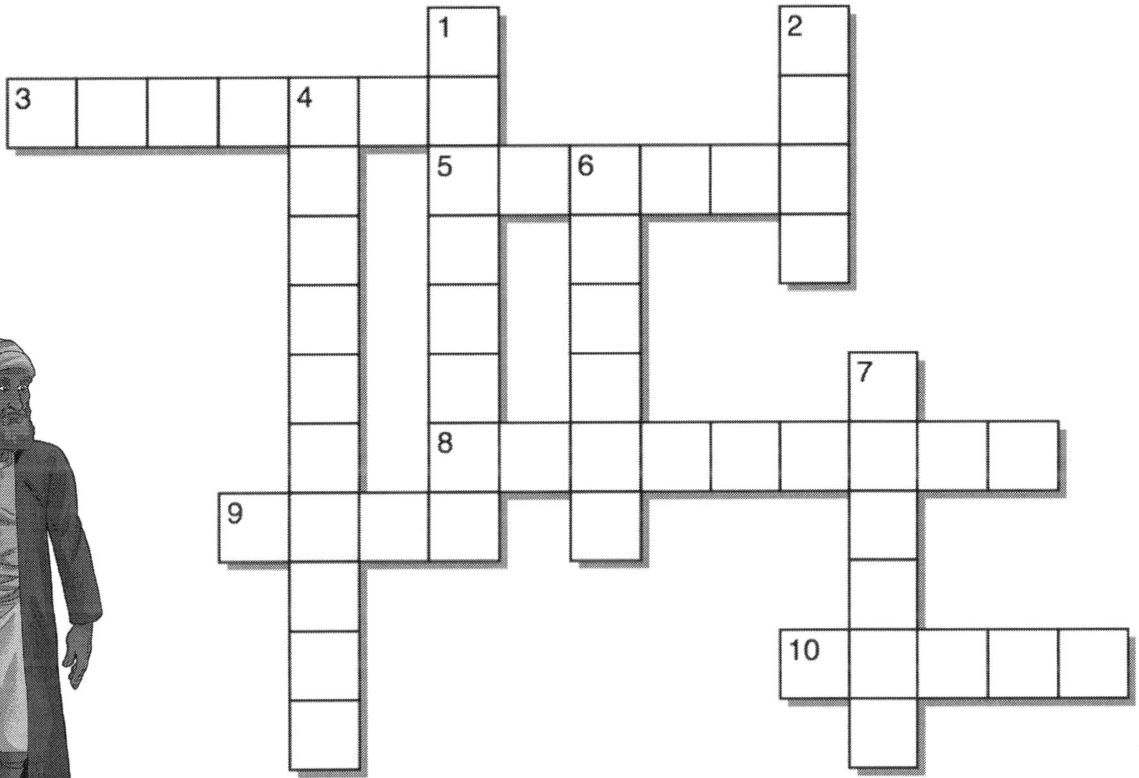

ACROSS

3) Men visited Jerusalem from _____, Cappadocia, Pontos, and Asia… (Acts 2:9)
5) During the Day of Pentecost, there were men from every _____. (Acts 2:5)
8) The men were amazed and said to each other, "look, aren't all these who speak_____. (Acts 2:7)
9) Tongues like _____ settled on each apostle. (Acts 2:3)
10) This apostle told the men of Israel to repent. (Acts 2:38)

DOWN

1) The people were confused because everyone heard the apostles speak in his own _____. (Acts 2:6)
2) Suddenly there came a sound from the heaven, like a mighty _____." (Acts 2:2)
4) The apostles were filled with this, and began to speak with other languages. (Acts 2:4)
6) The Temple was in this city.
7) "We hear them speaking in own language the great deeds of _____." (Acts 2:11)

"... there came from heaven a sound like a mighty rushing wind..."

(Acts 2:2)

The Holy Spirit

Read John 16:8. The role of the Holy Spirit is to….

Read 1 John 3:4. The Bible says that sin is…

The fruit of the Holy Spirit in my life is…

Read Deuteronomy 6:24-25. We are righteous if we…

City of Jerusalem

The Jerusalem News

ACTS 2 — DAY OF PENTECOST — A BIBLE HISTORY PUBLICATION

Day of worship

....

....

....

....

....

Israelites celebrate Shavu'ot

....

....

....

Pilgrims arrive!

TWELVE TRIBES OF ISRAEL

After capturing the land of Canaan, Joshua and the Israelites divided the land between the twelve tribes of Israel. After that time, Israelites came to Jerusalem every year to celebrate Shavu'ot. Using a historical atlas, write each tribe's name inside the correct boundary on the map.

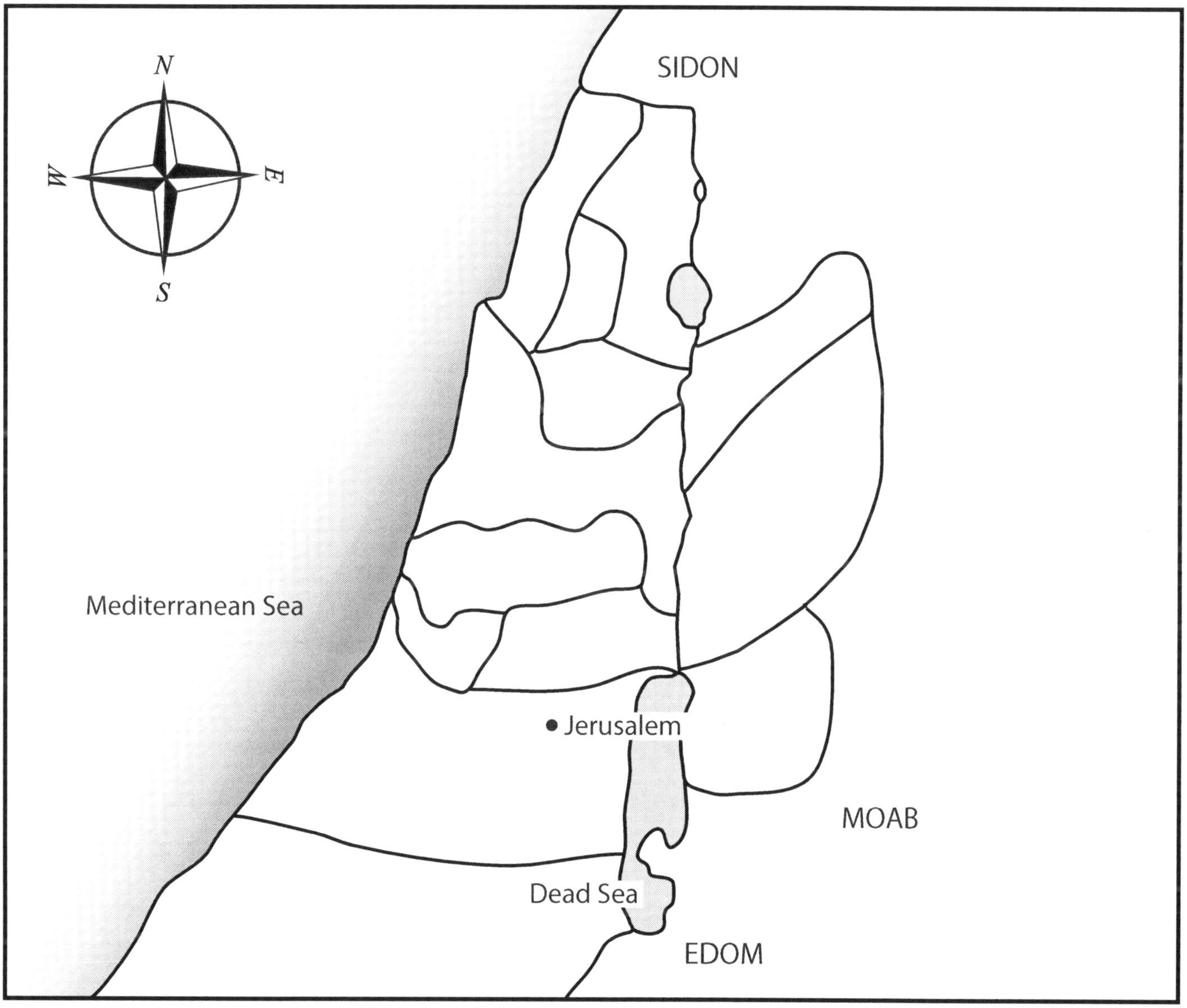

SIMEON	GAD	ISSACHAR	MANASSEH
JUDAH	DAN	ZEBULON	EPHRAIM
REUBEN	ASHER	NEPHTALI	BENJAMIN

Peter

Read Acts 2:14-41 and write a summary of Peter's speech below.

....

....

....

1. Who did Peter speak to?
....
....

2. Who did Yah raise up?
....
....

3. What did Peter tell the men to do in Acts 2:38?
....
....

Draw a scene from this Bible passage.

What could the life of Peter teach me?	Yah used Peter to...

SHAVU'OT

Read Exodus 20 and Acts 1-3.
Find and circle each of the words from the list below.

```
P I L G R I M A G E S P G H X H
B A I M V N Q R C B L E T G H L
Y P S H R A Q S R Q A N O X Z O
O P R H O Q P Z Y O N T R Q E G
Y O A I A V M M O H G E A D J A
W I E V E V E G P S U C H U B P
Y N L H U S U U D O A O R J J O
A T I B C G T O W M G S K N W S
H E T O B L N F T P E T M G B T
W D E Z H P M A I O S P A V Z L
E T S P H O L Y S P I R I T W E
H I V J E R U S A L E M R W J S
H M Z V K M O U N T S I N A I U
N E X K F O S L T F M O S E S J
H A R V E S T N F U E B Y H X K
Y T E M P L E T V A Z X I L W U
```

SHAVUOT	MOUNT SINAI	TEMPLE	PRIEST
APOSTLES	LANGUAGES	YAHWEH	PENTECOST
PILGRIMAGE	TORAH	ISRAELITES	MOSES
HOLY SPIRIT	HARVEST	JERUSALEM	APPOINTED TIME

How many people were baptized (mikvah'd) on Shavu'ot?

Unscramble the words to find the answer. *Hint: Read Acts 2:41 (ESV).*

Toseh woh gadlyl cirdveee ish

_____

rowd were pedzitab. ehrTe

_____

erew dadde htat yda tuabo

_____

erhte odtsnahu sulos.

_____

EXTRA ACTIVITIES

PLAGUE OF BLOOD!

Open your Bible and read Exodus 7:1-25. Write a description of the plague of blood. Color the illustration at the bottom of the page.

PLAGUE OF FROGS!

Open your Bible and read Exodus 8:1-15. Write a description of the plague of frogs. Color the illustration at the bottom of the page.

PLAGUE OF LICE!

Open your Bible and read Exodus 8:16-19. Write a description of the plague of lice. Color the illustration at the bottom of the page.

PLAGUE OF FLIES!

Open your Bible and read Exodus 8:20-32. Write a description of the plague of flies. Color the illustration at the bottom of the page.

EGYPTIAN LIVESTOCK DIE!

Open your Bible and read Exodus 9:1-7. Write a description of the plague of cattle. Color the illustration at the bottom of the page.

PLAGUE OF BOILS!

Open your Bible and read Exodus 9:8-12. Write a description of the plague of boils. Color the illustration at the bottom of the page.

PLAGUE OF HAIL!

Open your Bible and read Exodus 9:22-26. Write a description of the plague of hail. Color the illustration at the bottom of the page.

PLAGUE OF LOCUSTS!

Open your Bible and read Exodus 10:12-20. Write a description of the plague of locusts. Color the illustration at the bottom of the page.

PLAGUE OF DARKNESS!

Open your Bible and read Exodus 10:21-29. Write a description of the plague of darkness. Color the illustration at the bottom of the page.

DEATH OF THE FIRSTBORN!

Open your Bible and read Exodus 11-12. Write a description of the death of the firstborn. Color the illustration at the bottom of the page.

CRAFTS & PROJECTS

Make a Paper Plate Lamb

You will need:
1. Paper plates
2. White cotton balls
3. Black construction paper
4. Craft animal eyes
5. School glue

Preparation:
Cut out the sheep face, legs, and ears from the template on the next page.

Instructions:

1. Cover a paper plate with school glue.
2. Cover the school glue with white cotton balls.
3. Help your child assemble the sheep's face using the sheep template pieces and craft eyes.
4. Glue the sheep's head and legs to the cotton ball body.

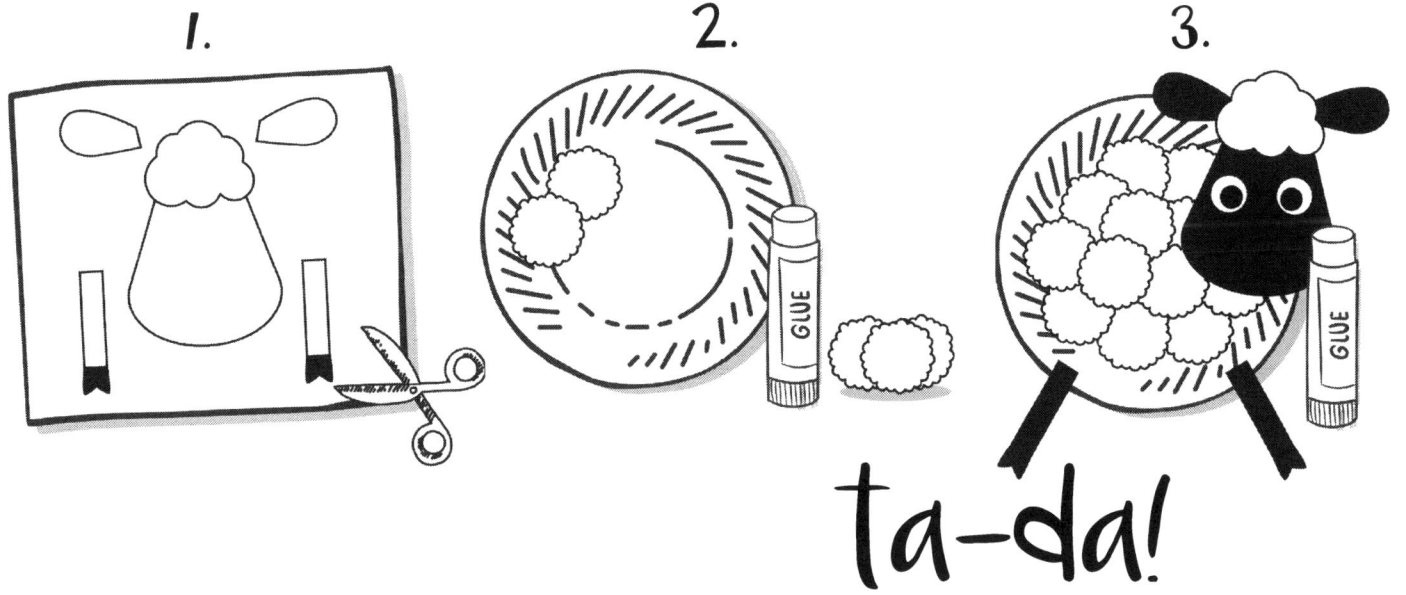

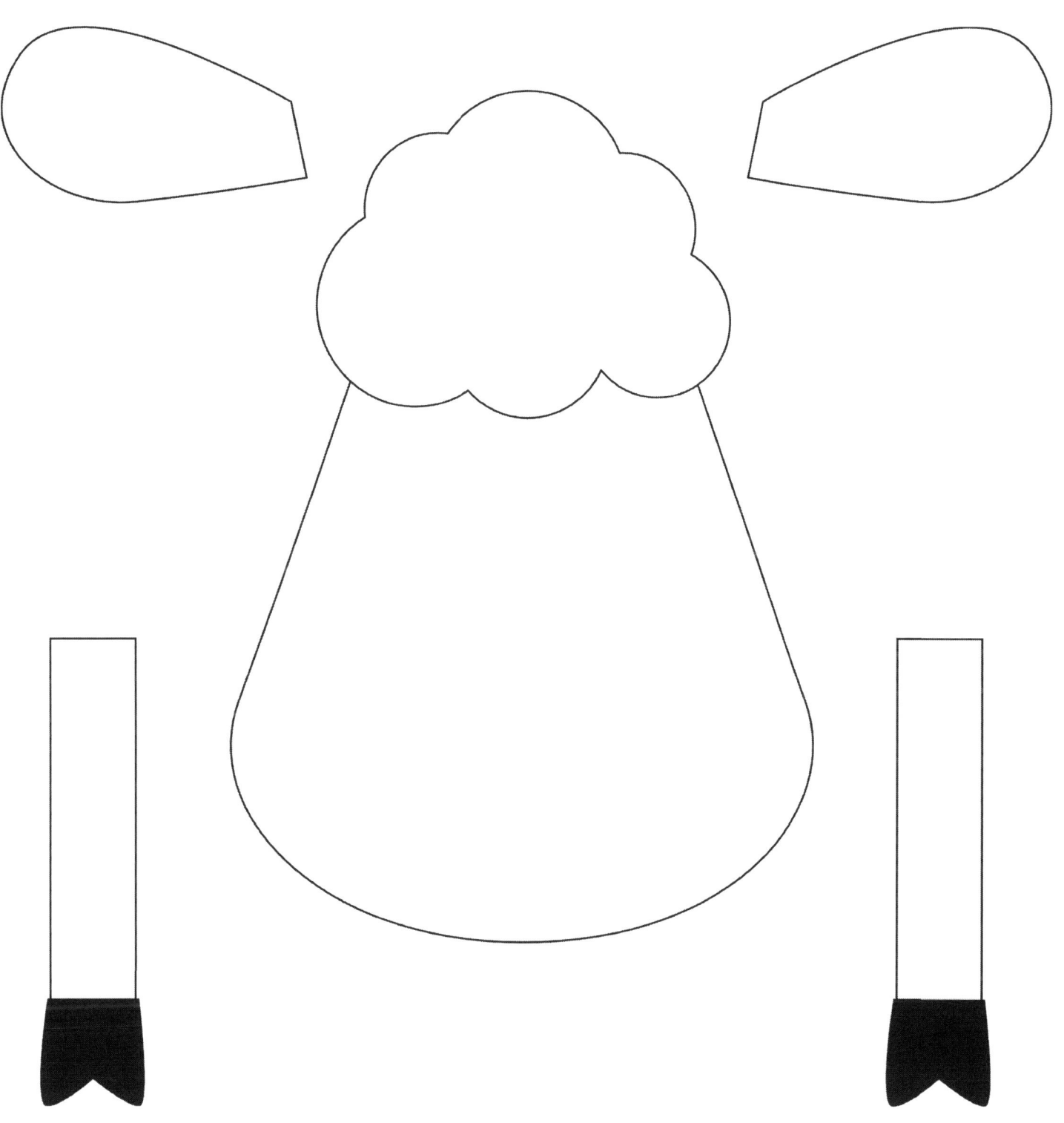

GARDEN OF GETHSEMANE

Before Yeshua died, He spent time in the garden with His disciples. Color and cut out Yeshua and the disciples. Place them in the garden.

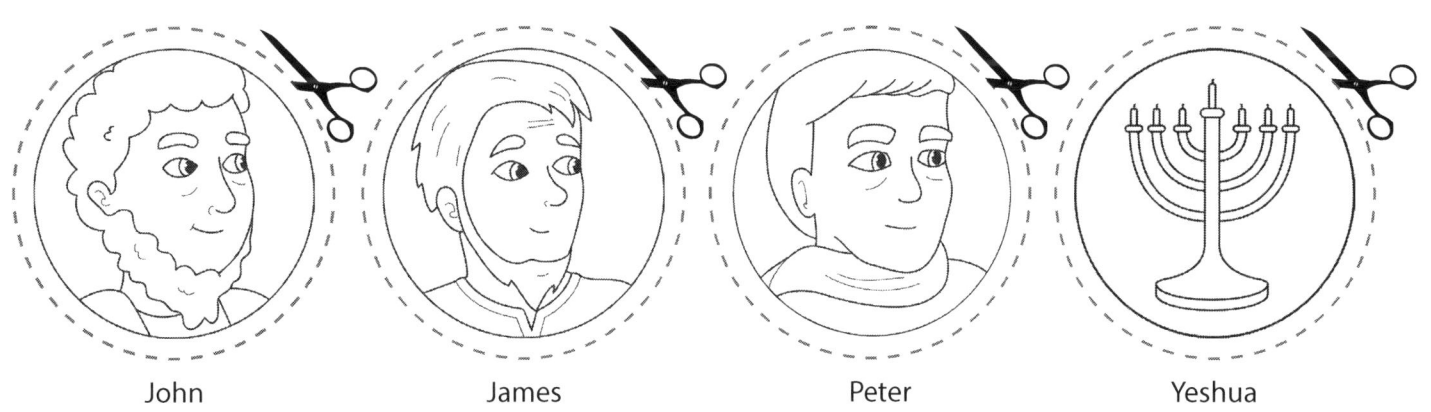

John　　　James　　　Peter　　　Yeshua

WHO SAID IT?

Read Luke 23, Matthew 26, and John 19. Color and cut out each Bible character. Match the quote with the person who said it.

1. "Father, forgive them, for they do not know what they are doing." – Luke 23:34

2. "I adjure You by the living God, that You tell us whether You are the Christ, the Son of God." – Matthew 26:63

3. "I do not know the man." – Matthew 26:72

4. "Take him yourselves and crucify him. I find no guilt in him." – John 19:6

Pilate   Caiaphas   Peter   Yeshua

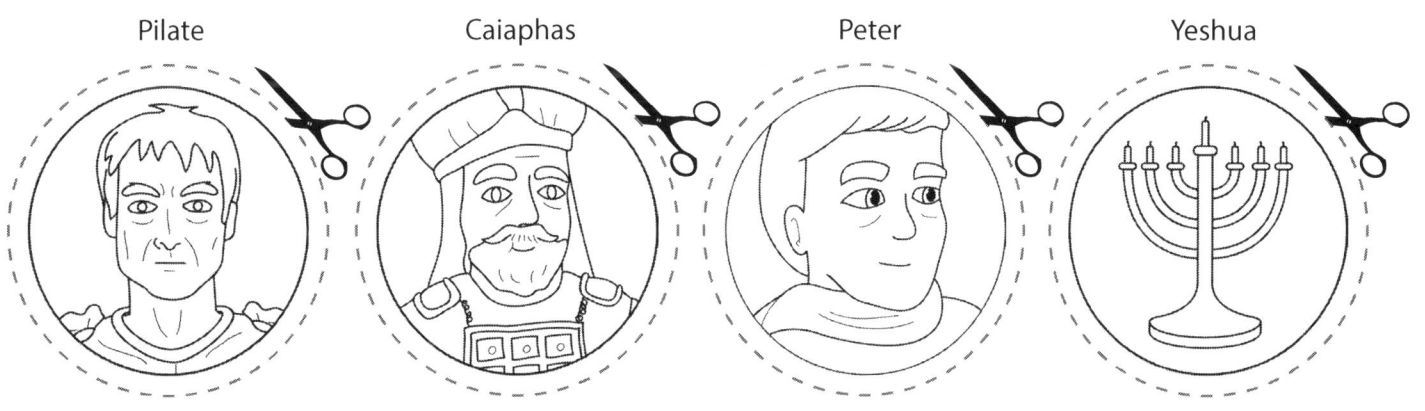

What goes inside the Temple?

You will need:
1. Scissors (adults-only)
2. Crayons, felt pens, or colored pencils
3. School glue

Instructions:

1. Cut out the template on the next page.
2. Color and cut out the temple objects on the following page. Paste each object inside the correct square on the template.

1.

2.
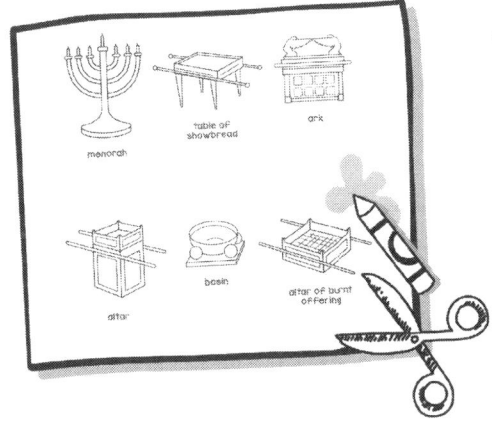

3.
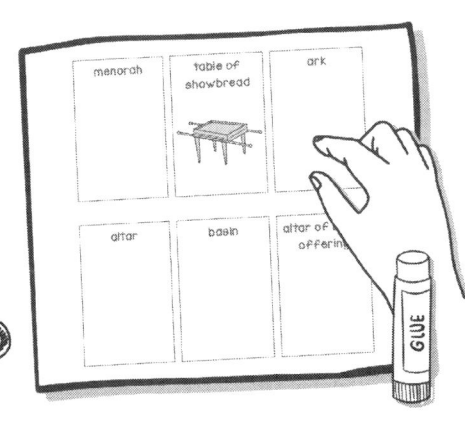

ta-da!

menorah	table of showbread	ark
altar	basin	altar of burnt offering

menorah · table of showbread · ark

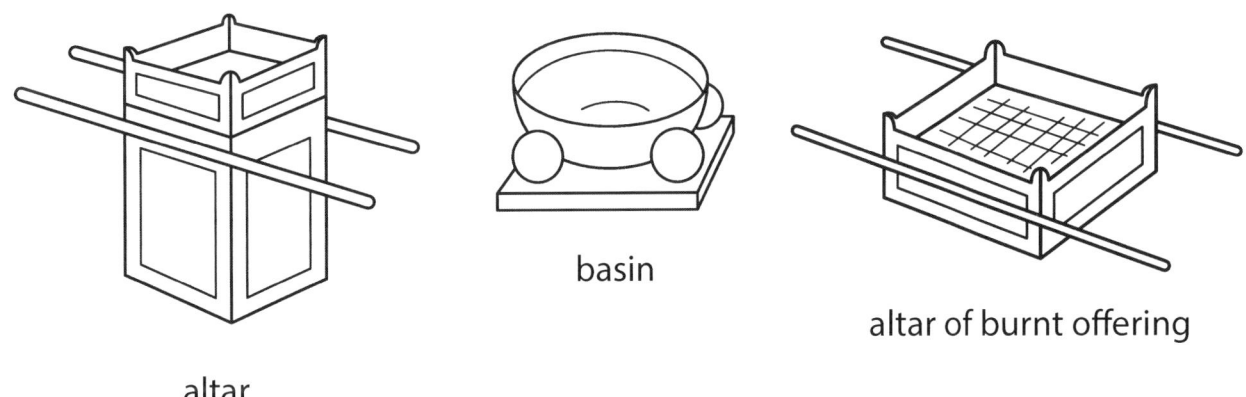

altar · basin · altar of burnt offering

Make a Paper Plate Tomb

You will need:
1. Two thick foam or paper plates (use the sturdy kind with a "lip")
2. Heavy card stock
3. Grey paint or crayons
4. Yeshua and the angel Bible characters (see next page)
5. Scissors (adult only)
6. Extra-strength glue sticks or School glue

Preparation:
Print the Yeshua and angel bible characters. Make copies onto heavy card stock and cut out the characters.

Instructions:

1. Cut the bottoms off both paper plates so they can stand up.
2. Paint or color the paper plates grey. Remember to color the front and back!
3. While the paper plate is drying, ask the children to color Yeshua and the angel.
4. Cut out a door on one paper plate. Glue both paper plates together to form a tomb.
5. Glue your cardboard Yeshua and angel onto the tomb.

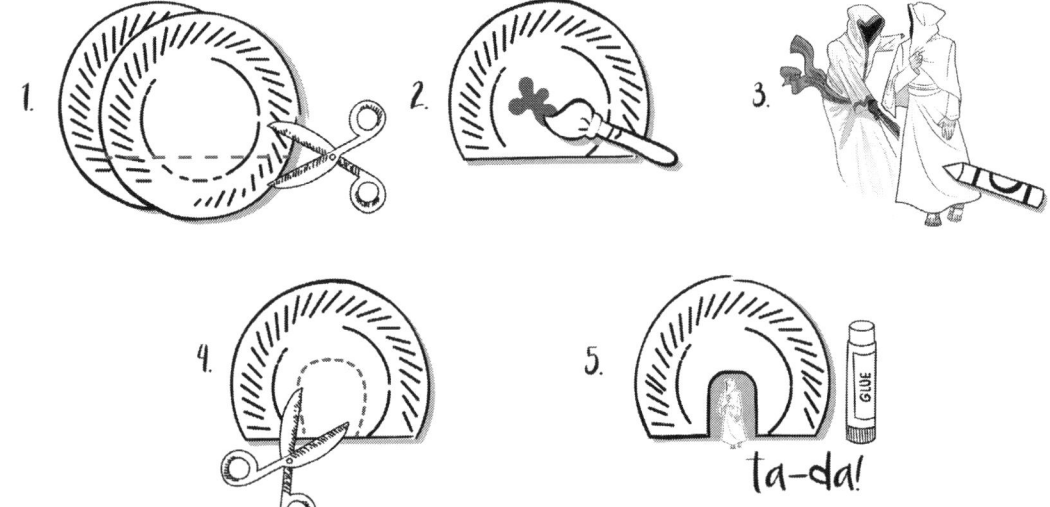

Bible characters: Yeshua and the angel.

The Ten Commandments Craft

Instructions:

There are two sections to this craft:
1. Ten Commandments
2. Two Tablets

You will need:
1. Grey paint or crayons
2. Felt pens, crayons or coloring pencils
3. Scissors (adult only)
4. Extra-strength glue sticks or School glue

Instructions:

1. Color the Ten Commandments circles on the following pages.
2. Print out the two tablets and Ten Commandments pages.
3. Cut out each commandment around the dotted edges.
4. Glue the tablets together by placing glue along the 'Glue Here' flap and sealing together.
5. Glue the commandments in numerical order onto the two stone tablets – five on each side.

Ta-da! Your very own Ten Commandments.

I AM YAH YOUR GOD

YOU SHALL HAVE NO OTHER GODS BEFORE ME

YOU SHALL NOT TAKE THE NAME OF YAH IN VAIN

REMEMBER THE SABBATH

HONOR YOUR FATHER AND MOTHER

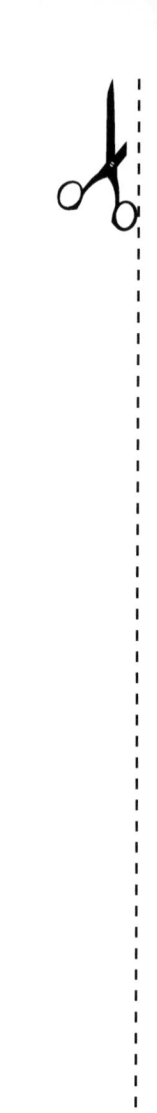

YOU SHALL NOT MURDER

YOU SHALL NOT COMMIT ADULTERY

YOU SHALL NOT STEAL

YOU SHALL NOT BEAR FALSE TESTIMONY AGAINST YOUR NEIGHBOR

YOU SHALL NOT COVET YOUR NEIGHBOR'S THINGS

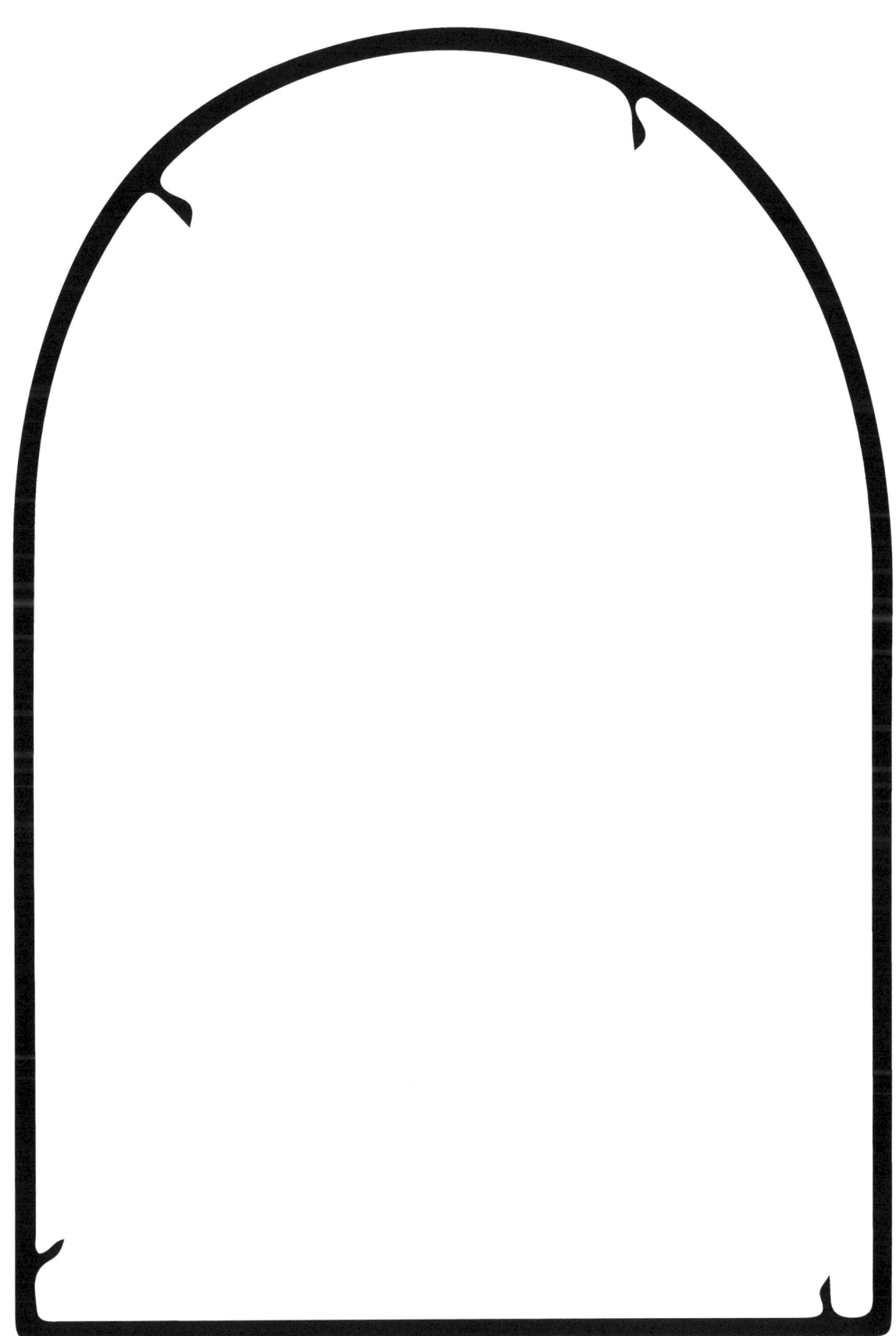

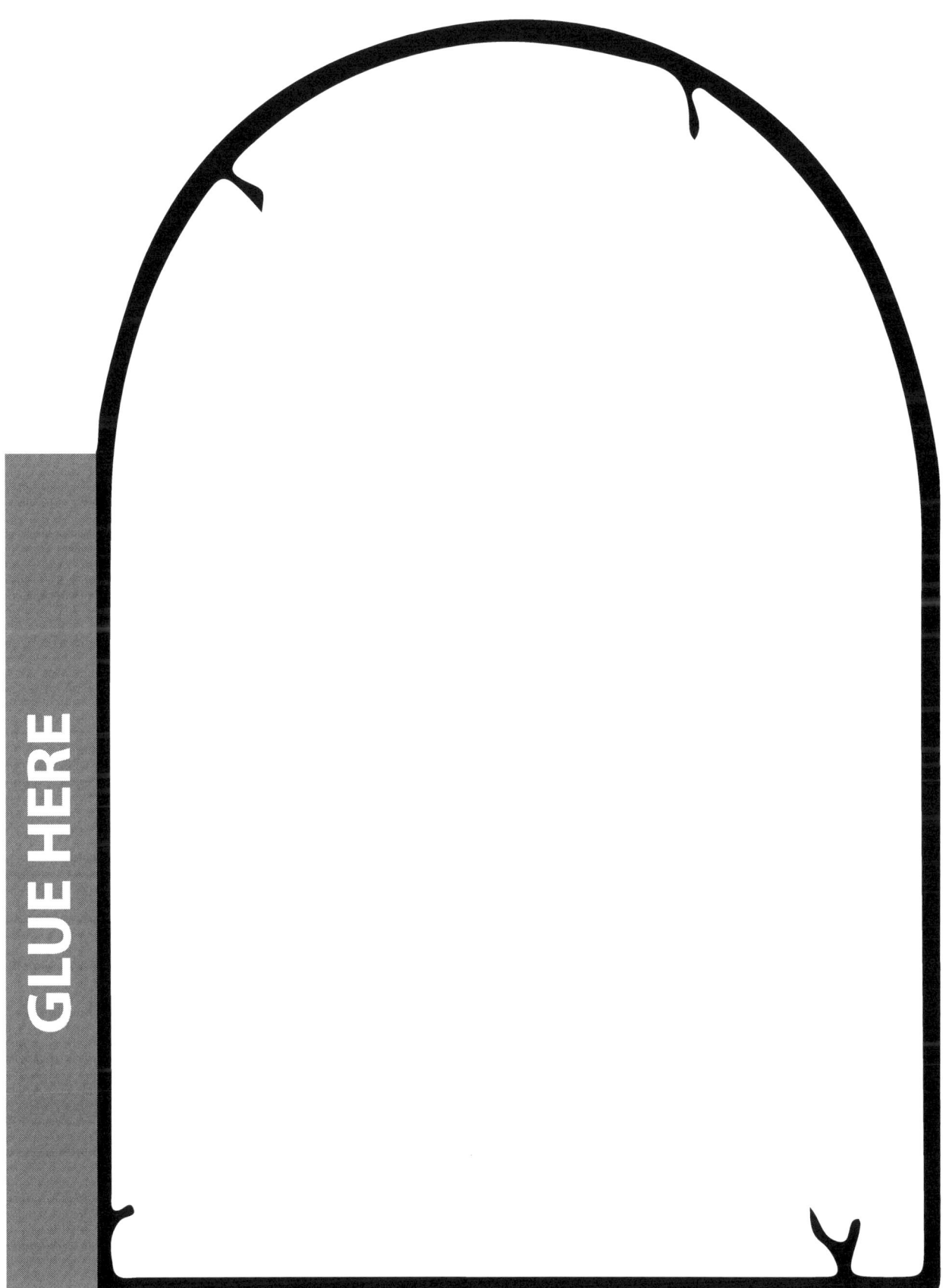

SHAVU'OT IN JERUSALEM

On Shavu'ot, Peter, the disciples, and Israelites from places like Mesopotamia and Parthia gathered together to honor this Appointed Time. Color and cut out the people. Place them in the temple.

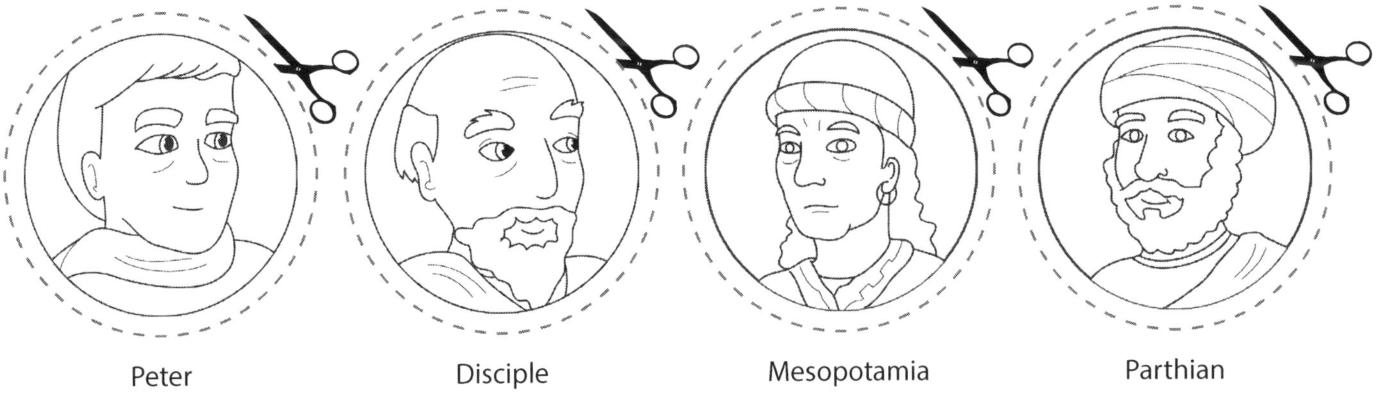

| Peter | Disciple | Mesopotamia | Parthian |

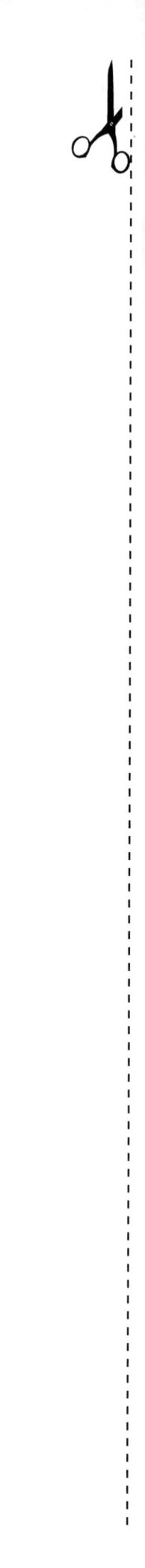

SHAVU'OT

Read Leviticus 23 and Acts 2. Discuss how the pictures below relate to Shavu'ot. Cut out a word or phrase at the bottom of the page. Match it with the correct picture.

wind | Israel | temple | mikveh

grain | God's people | Sabbath

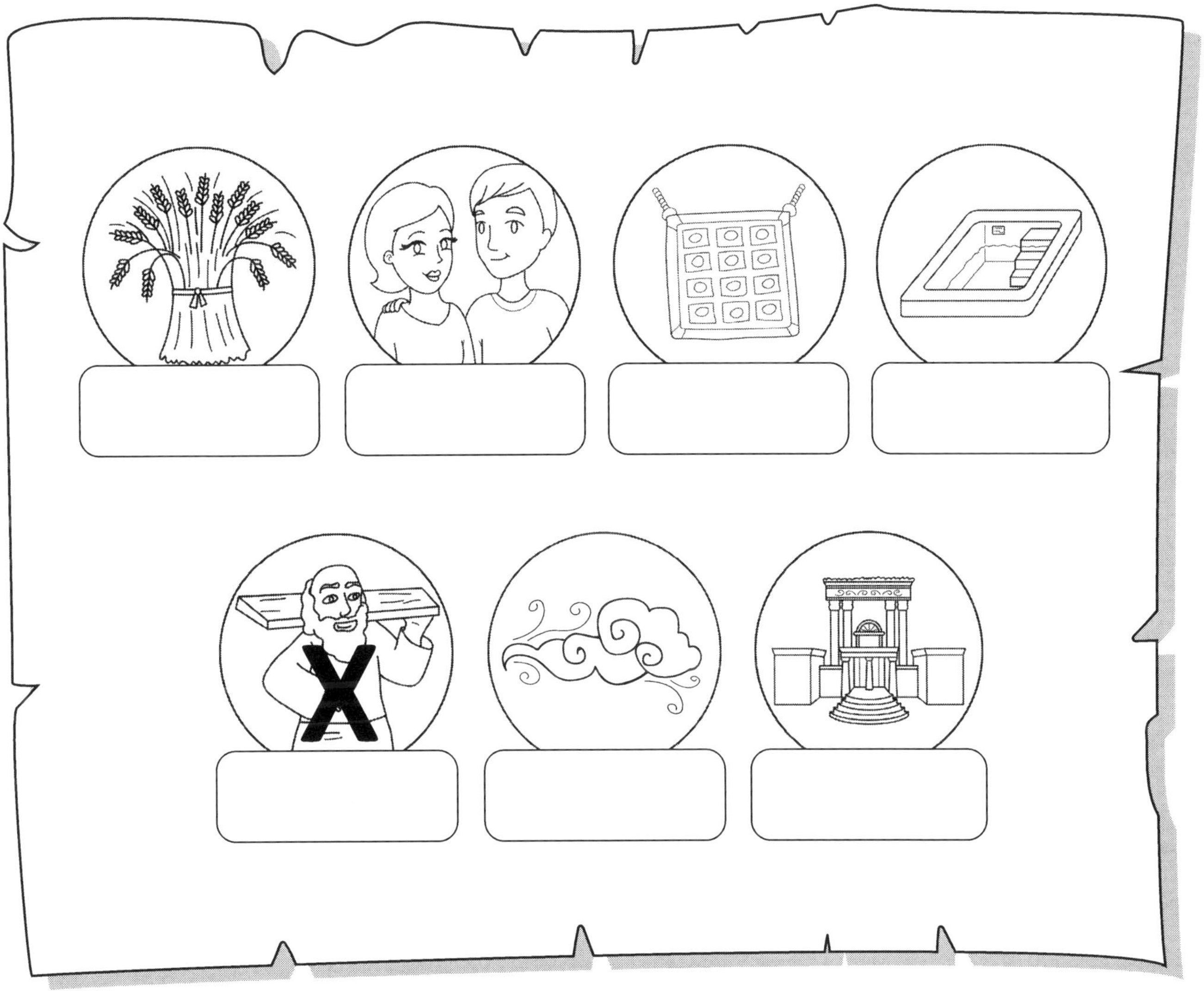

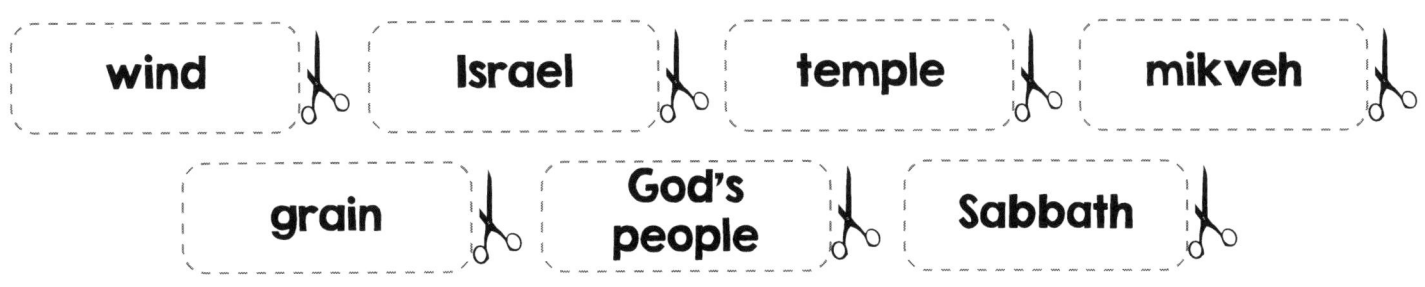

Make an Appointed Times mobile

You will need:

1. Card stock
2. Paint, felt pens, or crayons
3. String
4. Scissors (adult only)
5. Glue stick or tape
6. Wooden sticks

Instructions:

1. Ask your children to color the Appointed Times circles on the next page.
2. When your children have finished drawing, cut out the mobile pieces and glue onto heavy card stock. Wait for the glue to dry.
3. Carefully cut out the mobile pieces.
4. Make a hole at the top of each mobile piece, string the pieces together, and attach to a piece of wood.

ta-da!

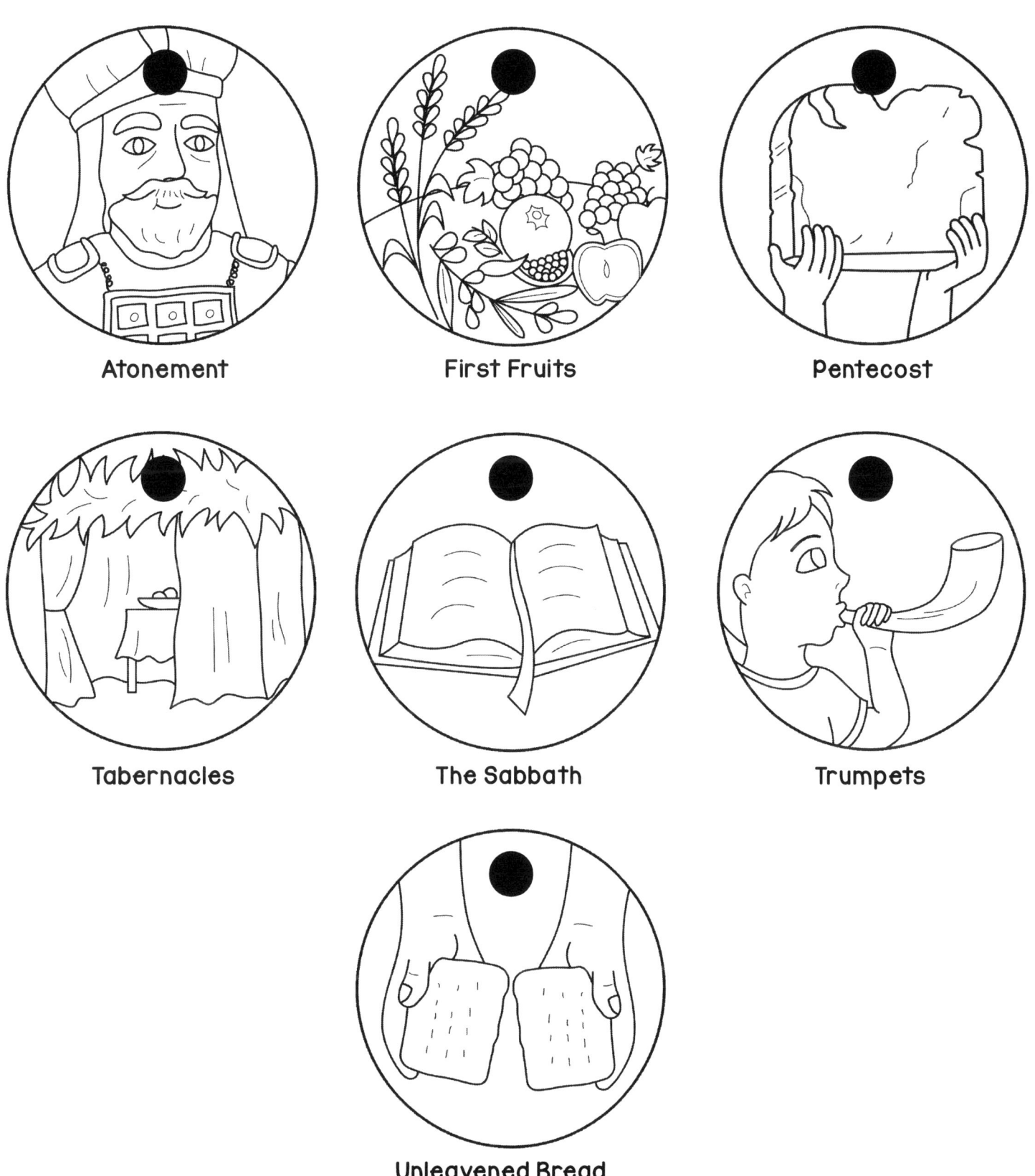

ANSWER KEY

The Passover & Feast of Unleavened Bread (Pesach & Chag HaMatzot)

Bible quiz: The Ten Plagues
1. Water turns into blood
2. Turning water into blood, and frogs
3. Flies
4. Boils
5. Darkness
6. Death of the firstborn
7. Ten
8. Yah
9. Joseph
10. Unleavened Bread

Bible crossword: The Passover
Across:
2. lamb
4. Moses
7. scripture
9. Unleavened Bread

Down:
1. Passover
3. bones
5. Yeshua
6. blood
8. Pharaoh
10. leaven

Comprehension worksheet: The Passover meal
Suggested answers:
1. Yah could show how powerless the Egyptians' false gods were compared to Him
2. Lamb, bitter herbs, and bread. Or something else?

Bible word search: Unleavened Bread

What's the Word?
This day shall be a memorial and you shall keep it as a feast to Yah: throughout your generations you shall keep it as feast forever. "'Seven days you shall eat unleavened bread; on the first day you shall put away yeast out of your houses, for whoever eats leavened bread from the first day until the seventh day shall be cut off from Israel. In the first day there shall be to you a holy convocation, and in the seventh day a holy convocation; no kind of work shall be done except that which every man must eat that may only be done by you. You shall observe the Appointed Time of Unleavened Bread; for in this same day have I brought your armies out of the land of Egypt: therefore observe this day throughout your generations forever. In the first month, on the fourteenth day of the month at evening, you shall eat unleavened bread until the twenty first day of the month at evening.

Fact sheet: Unleavened Bread
Answer to question #2:
Seven days you shall eat unleavened bread. On the first day you shall remove leaven out of your houses, for if anyone eats what is leavened, from the first day until the seventh day, that person shall be cut off from Israel. On the first day you shall hold a holy assembly, and on the seventh day a holy assembly. No work shall be done on those days. But what everyone needs to eat, that alone may be prepared by you. And you shall observe the Feast of Unleavened Bread, for on this very day I brought your hosts out of the land of Egypt. Therefore, you shall observe this day, throughout your generations, as a statute forever. In the first month, from the fourteenth day of the month at evening, you shall eat unleavened bread until the twenty-first day of the month at evening. For seven days no leaven is to be found in your houses. If anyone eats what is leavened, that person will be cut off from the congregation of Israel, whether he is a sojourner or a native of the land.

Coloring worksheet: Yeshua before Pilate
1. Yeshua remained silent
2. Pilate's wife sent him a message
3. Yeshua

Bible quiz: The Passover & Feast of Unleavened Bread
1. Feast of Unleavened Bread
2. Unleavened bread (bread without yeast)
3. Seven days
4. Feast of Unleavened Bread
5. Throughout their generations (forever)
6. King Hezekiah
7. Jerusalem
8. Troas
9. 5000
10. First Fruits

Bible quiz: Death on the stake
1. Pilate, the Roman Governor
2. Simon of Cyrene
3. Golgotha
4. King of the Judeans
5. My God, my God, why have you forsaken me?
6. Two criminals
7. Three hours
8. Nicodemus
9. Spear
10. Linen cloth

Coloring worksheet: Crucifixion
1. The curtain (veil) at the temple
2. An earthquake
3. The centurion and guards who were guarding Yeshua

Comprehension worksheet: The Temple
Suggested answers:
1. King Solomon
2. At the temple, Israelites who wanted to sacrifice a lamb formed groups. Each group slaughtered one Passover lamb for that group of people. The Passover lamb, unlike the usual animal offerings, was sacrificed by the Israelites themselves

Who said it?
1 = Yeshua, 2 = Caiaphas, 3 = Peter, 4 = Pilate

Feast of First Fruits (Bikkurim)
What's the Word?
Yah spoke to Moses, saying, "Speak to the children of Israel and tell them, 'When you have come into the land which I give to you and reap its harvest, then you shall bring the sheaf of the first fruits of your harvest to the priest: and he shall wave the sheaf before Yah, to be accepted for you. On the next day after the Sabbath the priest shall wave it. On the day when you wave the sheaf, you shall offer a male lamb without defect a year old for a burnt offering to Yah.

Bible crossword: The cross and empty tomb
Across:
4. Golgotha
7. Pilate
8. angel
9. First Fruits

Down:
1. Earthquake
2. Cross
3. Galilee
5. Judas
6. veil
7. Peter

Fact Sheet: Golgotha discovered?
Suggested answers:
1. Place of the Skull
2. The actual crucifixion site was under many feet of soil, with holes in the rock where crosses were erected, and niches in the rock wall behind where signs were placed. The central cross-hole had an earthquake crack beside it

Bible quiz: The Resurrection
1. An angel
2. First Fruits, during the week of Unleavened Bread
3. Money
4. Mary Magdalene
5. An empty tomb
6. "Why do you seek the living among the dead? 6 He is not here, but has risen."
7. Thomas
8. Sea of Galilee
9. 40 days (Acts 1:3)
10. Go and make disciples

Bible word search: The Resurrection

Coloring worksheet: First Fruits
1. An angel of God
2. Mary Magdalene
3. The disciples

Disciple Facts
Andrew = 6, Bartholomew = 9, James, son of Zebedee = 5, Judas = 1, John = 3, Jude = 8, Matthew = 7, Peter = 10, Philip = 4, Thomas = 2

Comprehension worksheet: The Romans
Suggested answers:
1. The Romans used crucifixion as a way to control everyone
2. The Hebrews had to pay food, road, poll, religious, water, house, and sales taxes, and extra taxes on items such as meat and salt

Question 'n color: The guard's report
1. A group of Roman soldiers
2. A bribe (money)
3. His disciples came by night and stole him away while we were asleep

Bible quiz: The twelve disciples
1. Matthew
2. Simon (Peter) and Andrew
3. Peter
4. The last supper in the upper room in Jerusalem
5. Judas
6. Transfiguration
7. Washed their feet
8. John
9. Go and make disciples
10. Donkey and colt

Comprehension worksheet: Who was Pontius Pilate?
Suggested answers:
1. Pilate was accused of harsh behavior, pride, violence, greed, holding executions without trial, and horrible cruelty towards the Hebrew people
2. A limestone block with an inscription that says, "Pontius Pilate, Prefect of Judea."

Day of Pentecost (Shavu'ot)
Bible quiz: The Ten Commandments
1. Moses and the Israelites
2. Honor your father and mother
3. 6th commandment
4. Two tablets of stone
5. Remember the Sabbath
6. 9th commandment
7. 8th commandment
8. 2nd commandment
9. Mount Sinai
10. Do not desire your neighbor's possessions

Question 'n color: Mount Sinai
1. The Sabbath
2. Our mother and father
3. The Israelites were afraid they would die

Bible quiz: Shavu'ot
1. Mount Sinai
2. Forty days and nights
3. Twelve tribes of Israel
4. Remember the Sabbath and keep it holy
5. Honor your father and mother
6. A sound from heaven like rushing wind
7. Each person heard the disciples speaking to them in their own language
8. Peter
9. About three thousand people
10. Ten

What's the Word?
Now when the day of Pentecost had come, they were all in one place. Suddenly there came from the sky a sound like a rushing mighty wind, and it filled the entire house where they were sitting. Tongues like fire appeared and were distributed to them, and one sat on each of them. They were all filled with the Holy Spirit and began to speak in other languages, as the Spirit gave them the ability to speak. Now there were dwelling in Jerusalem Israelites, devout men, from every nation under the sky. When this sound was heard, the crowd came together and were surprised, because everyone heard the apostles speaking in his own language. They were all amazed, saying to one another, "Aren't these men who speak from the Galilee? How do we hear everyone in our own native language? Parthians, Medes, Elamites, and people from Mesopotamia, Judea, Cappadocia, Pontus, Asia, Phrygia, Pamphylia, Egypt, the parts of Libya around Cyrene, visitors from Rome, both Jews and proselytes, Cretans and Arabians: we hear them speaking in our languages the mighty works of God!"

Bible crossword: Shavu'ot
Across:
3. Parthia
5. nation
8. Galileans
9. fire
10. Peter

Down:
1. language
2. wind
4. Holy Spirit
6. Jerusalem
7. Yahweh

Map activity: Twelve tribes of Israel

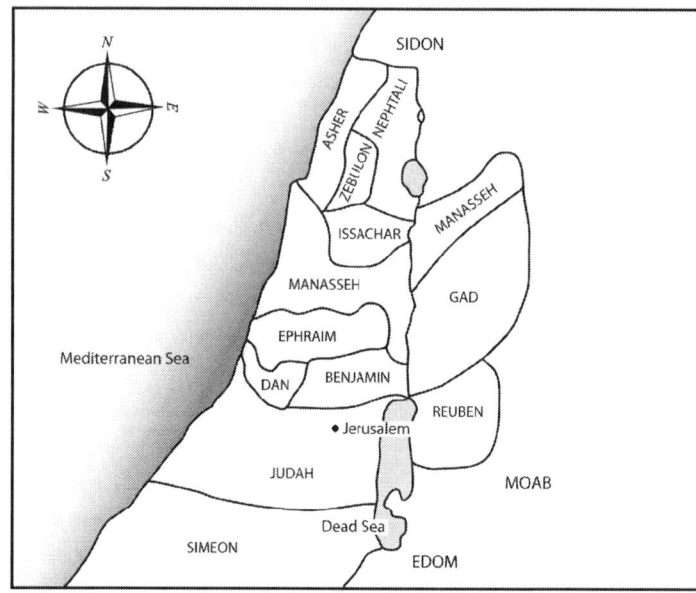

Coloring worksheet: Peter
1. Men of Judea and men of Israel
2. Yeshua
3. Repent and be baptized in the name of Yeshua

Shavu'ot Word Search

Bible word scramble: How many people were baptized (mikvah'd)?
Those who gladly received his word were baptized. There were added that day about three thousand souls

◆◇ DISCOVER MORE ACTIVITY BOOKS! ◇◆

Available for purchase at www.biblepathwayadventures.com

INSTANT DOWNLOAD!

100 Bible Quizzes	The Spring Feasts (Beginners)
Moses Ten Plagues	Moses Ten Plagues (Beginners)
The Exodus	The Exodus (Beginners)
The Fall Feasts	The Spring Feasts

Made in the USA
Middletown, DE
04 April 2021